SHAKESPEARE ON STAGE

AS YOU LIKE IT

HAMLET

JULIUS CAESAR

MACBETH

THE MERCHANT OF VENICE

A MIDSUMMER NIGHT'S DREAM

OTHELLO, THE MOOR OF VENICE

ROMEO AND JULIET

SHAKESPEARE FOR YOUNG PEOPLE

HAMLET

HENRY THE FIFTH

JULIUS CAESAR

MACBETH

A MIDSUMMER NIGHT'S DREAM

MUCH ADO ABOUT NOTHING

ROMEO AND JULIET

THE TAMING OF THE SHREW

THE TEMPEST

TWELFTH NIGHT

D0720702

SHAKESPEARE ON STAGE

A
MIDSUMMER
NIGHT'S
DREAM

by
William Shakespeare

edited and illustrated by
Diane Davidson

SWAN BOOKS
A division of Learning Links Inc.
New Hyde Park, New York

Published by:

SWAN BOOKS
a division of
LEARNING LINKS INC.
2300 Marcus Avenue
New Hyde Park, NY 11042

Printed in the United States of America

Library of Congress Cataloging-in-Publication Data

Shakespeare, William, 1564-1616.
   A Midsummer Night's Dream

    (Shakespeare on stage)
    I. Davidson, Diane. II. Title. III. Series:
Shakespeare, William, 1564-1616. Shakespeare on
stage.
PR2878.08D38   1985   822.3'3   83-60730
ISBN 0-7675-0868-8

FOREWORD TO THE SERIES

Sometimes, in our desire to appreciate Shakespeare properly, we forget the obvious: that Shakespeare was not a schoolteacher, not a classical scholar, but a professional entertainer. He made his chief living in the theatre as an actor and producer. There is no evidence that he helped his fellow-actors Heminge and Condell preserve his works in print for readers. The plays were written to be heard and seen.

I prepared this adaption, cutting the text to suit an average audience, supplying the missing visual effects by descriptions, and adding explanatory notes in parentheses where necessary. The awkward ten-syllable printed line has been discarded, as it does not appear in a living theatre production. Shakespeare's words, however, are not changed. But my efforts thus are incomplete. The plays should also be read aloud with a group of friends, for Shakespeare's words feel good inside the mouth, and his sounds are a delight to any ear. A great writer should be enjoyed with all the senses.

I described my approach to a friend.

"But you're not really changing Shakespeare," he said. "You're just directing his shows on paper."

"Yes," I answered, "that's my intent — to give his spoken words a natural background."

Perhaps Will himself would not be too displeased. To his Elizabethan age, a play was play, not work.

And so I think it sensible at first for people to read shortened versions of Shakespeare's plays, with immediate explanations, in order to become familiar with the stories and major scenes. Also the reader begins to tune his ears to Shakespeare's speech. Later, we gain even more enjoyment from the uncut manuscripts and from different interpretations, especially on the stage. But however we approach Shakespeare's great plays, we should take pleasure in them.

Diane Davidson

Fair Oaks, California
1985

A MIDSUMMER NIGHT'S DREAM

CHARACTERS

Members of the Duke's Court

Theseus, Duke of Athens, a Greek hero

Hippolyta, Queen of the Amazons, the Duke's bride

Egeus, an old courtier and a stern father

Hermia, a little brunette, daughter to Egeus, in love with Lysander

Lysander, a noble youth in love with Hermia

Demetrius, a noble but selfish youth, also in love with Hermia

Helena, a tall blonde, the schoolgirl friend of Hermia, in love with Demetrius, her former fiance.

Philostrate, the Master of Revels, in charge of all entertainment at the Duke's court

Courtiers, Attendants, Foresters, etc.

Workmen of Athens Who Act in the Amateur Play

Peter Quince, the director and author of the play

Bottom, the over-enthusiastic hero of the play

Flute, a skinny youth who is embarrassed to play the heroine

Snug, a slow-witted carpenter who plays the lion

Snout, a practical repairman who plays a stone wall

Starveling, a timid tailor who plays the Man in the Moon

Fairy Folk

Oberon, King of Faerie, handsome, dark and
    jealous
Titania, the lovely winged Queen of Faerie
A little Indian page boy
Puck, a mischievous goblin, a servant of Oberon
Peaseblossom ⎫
Mustardseed ⎬ Fairies in
Cobweb   ⎬ attendance
Moth   ⎭ on Titania
Other Fairies, Sprites, Goblins, Elves, etc.

THE BACKGROUND
OF THE PLAY

A Midsummer Night's Dream is made of fantasy and fun. Its purpose is entertainment only, and if it preaches a moral, it is merely Puck's exclamation, "Lord, what fools these mortals be!" Yet the mortals are not the only fools in the play, for Puck, the mischievous goblin from the land of Faerie, causes as many problems as the human characters from Athens.

In this story, Athens is not the real Athens of Greece or even of mythology; it is a charming Never-Never Land of Poetry. There, people are idealized figures from medieval romance, including the majestic Duke Theseus and his stately bride-to-be, Hippolyta, the Queen of the Amazons. Although recently at war with each other, these two rulers have found that love solves all conflicts, and their wedding provides the background against which the three plots of the play are presented.

The first story concerns two girls: Hermia, a little brunette, and her best friend, Helena, a tall blonde. Hermia is engaged secretly to Lysander, but she is also persistently wooed by Demetrius, another noble youth. These two young men seem so alike that few people can keep their identities separate without the aid of a memory device, such as nicknaming one "Loving Lysander" and the other "Demanding Demetrius." Into their lives come complications from Egeus,

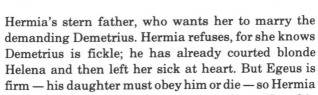

Hermia's stern father, who wants her to marry the demanding Demetrius. Hermia refuses, for she knows Demetrius is fickle; he has already courted blonde Helena and then left her sick at heart. But Egeus is firm — his daughter must obey him or die — so Hermia and her loving Lysander agree to elope. For this purpose they will meet in a magic wood outside of Athens.

At the same time, a group of craftsmen in Athens, resembling strongly the workmen of Shakespeare's England, plan to rehearse a home-made play for the Duke's wedding entertainment. If chosen to perform at the palace, they can be sure of a rich reward. Unfortunately, no one is aware the play is an amateur disaster. Full of enthusiasm, the workingmen decide to go to the magic wood outside of Athens to rehearse apart from curious eyes.

The third plot concerns the inhabitants of the mystic wood, the spirits of Faerie. These elves are part of the Celtic tradition of folklore that is native to Ireland, England and France especially. The Celts believed in a bright and sometimes frightening Otherworld of magic, adventure and romance. In modern books this idea reappears as Tolkien's Middle Earth and C. S. Lewis's Narnia, still as enchanting as in Elizabethan times. However, Shakespeare's audience shared one belief not held today: that especially on Midsummer's Eve, the sprites of Fairyland come out to walk the earth with mortal folk. On this special night, much of our play takes place.

When the curtain rises on the fantasy, we see the gracious court of Athens with the royal lovers, Theseus

and Hippolyta, looking forward to their wedding in a few short days. But a cloud appears when Old Egeus comes in to complain that his stubborn daughter will not marry the man he has chosen for her. Thus the midsummer's tale begins.

ACT I

Scene 1

(On a night late in June, faint moonlight falls on the great staircase of the white marble palace at Athens. Duke Theseus enters with his bride-to-be, the lovely Amazon Queen Hippolyta. She wears a crescent moon in her crown, for she is a follower of Diana, the goddess of the moon and of hunting. In the darkness, courtiers follow them with torches. The light flickers on the handsome couple clad in royal robes that half-suggest the armor of their days of warfare. With a smile, Theseus embraces Hippolyta, as their wedding time is soon.)

Theseus: Now, fair Hippolyta, our nuptial hour draws on apace. Four happy days bring in another moon. *(He looks impatiently at the sky, where the old moon lingers and the new moon will announce their wedding night.)* But, O, methinks how slow this old moon wanes!

Hippolyta: (With a smile, knowing the thin new moon will soon appear.) Four days will quickly steep themselves in night, four nights will quickly dream away the time — and then the moon, like to a silver bow new-bent in heaven, shall behold the night of our solemnities.

Theseus: (To the Master of Revels, who arranges entertainment.) Go, Philostrate, stir up the Athenian

●≈≈≈≈≈≈≈≈≈≈≈≈≈≈≈≈≈≈≈≈≈≈≈≈≈≈≈≈≈●

youth to merriments! Awake the pert and nimble spirit of mirth! *(Philostrate bows and leaves as Theseus turns to his bride with loving promises of celebration.)* Hippolyta, I wooed thee with my sword, and won thy love doing thee injuries. But I will wed thee in another key — with pomp, with triumph and with reveling! *(But his joyful plans are interrupted by Egeus, a sour old courtier, who enters with his pretty little daughter Hermia. Two young men follow them — "Loving Lysander" and "Demanding Demetrius." Hermia, glancing at Lysander, has trouble keeping back the tears in her large dark eyes.)*

Egeus: (Bowing) Happy be Theseus, our renowned Duke!

Theseus: Thanks, good Egeus. What's the news with thee?

Egeus: (In tones of fretful anger.) Full of vexation come I, with complaint against my child, my daughter Hermia. *(Hermia curtsies.)*

(Egeus motions to one of the young men.) Stand forth, Demetrius! *(Demetrius, a noble young man with a smug expression, bows to the Duke as Egeus continues.)* My noble lord, this man hath my consent to marry her.

(He motions to the other young man.) Stand forth, Lysander! *(Lysander, a handsome youth, comes forward, his eyes anxiously on Hermia, who blows him a kiss. Her father frowns.)* And, my gracious Duke, this man hath bewitched the bosom of my child. *(He lists the love-tricks that Lysander has*

Theseus: Hippolyta, I wooed thee with my
sword... But I will wed thee in
another key!

used to steal Hermia's heart.) Thou, thou,
Lysander, thou hast given her rhymes, and inter-
changed love-tokens with my child. Thou hast by
moonlight at her window sung! With cunning
hast thou filched my daughter's heart, turned
her obedience, which is due to me, to stubborn
harshness. *(Lysander smiles in the old man's face
and blows a kiss back to Hermia, who giggles.
Egeus turns helplessly to the Duke with a plea to
have Hermia obey him or die, as the law of the city
requires.)*

And, my gracious Duke, be it so she will not here
consent to marry with Demetrius, I beg the
ancient privilege of Athens: as she is mine, I may
"dispose of her," which shall be either to this
gentleman...*(He points to Demetrius.)*...or to her
death, according to our law! *(Young Hermia and
Lysander look stunned at her father's harsh
choice.)*

Theseus: *(Frowning, he tries to act as a calm judge to
uphold the local courts.)* What say you, Hermia?
Be advised, fair maid. To you, your father should
be as a god! Demetrius is a worthy gentleman.

Hermia: *(In tears)* So is Lysander!

Theseus: *(With sympathy he agrees.)* In himself he is.
*(Yet the Duke must support the father's power of
approval.)* But, wanting your father's voice, the
other...*(He points to Demetrius.)*...must be held
the worthier.

Hermia: *(Wishing her father saw her point of view.)* I
would my father looked but with my eyes.

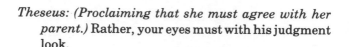

Theseus: (Proclaiming that she must agree with her parent.) Rather, your eyes must with his judgment look.

Hermia: (To everyone's surprise, even her own, she runs lightly forward to kneel at the Duke's feet.) I do entreat your Grace to pardon me. I know not by what power I am made bold. But I beseech your Grace that I may know the worst that may befall me in this case, if I refuse to wed Demetrius.

Theseus: (He holds a whispered consultation with Hippolyta, who touches the crescent moon of Diana in her crown. Nodding, he turns with a third choice for Hermia: to be a nun in the service of the virgin goddess Diana.) Either to die the death, or to abjure forever the society of men. Therefore, fair Hermia, question your desires — whether, if you yield not to your father's choice, you can endure the livery of a nun, to live a barren sister all your life, chanting faint hymns to the cold fruitless moon.

Hermia: (Rising, with a vow to be a nun rather than marry the wrong man.) So will I grow, so live, so die, my lord, ere I will yield unto his lordship! *(She throws a look of scorn at Demetrius.)*

Theseus: Take time to pause. And, by the next new moon...*(He takes Hippolyta's hand at the thought of their wedding.)*...the sealing-day betwixt my love and me, for everlasting bond of fellowship — upon that day, either prepare to die for disobedience to your father's will, or else to wed Demetrius, or on Diana's altar to protest for aye austerity and single life.

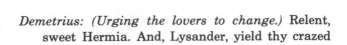

Demetrius: (Urging the lovers to change.) Relent, sweet Hermia. And, Lysander, yield thy crazed title to my certain right.

Lysander: You have her father's love, Demetrius. Let me have Hermia's. *(He laughs.)* You marry him!

Egeus: Scornful Lysander! True, he hath my love, and she is mine, and all my right of her I do estate unto Demetrius.

Lysander: (Kneeling before the Duke to plead his case, for he is equal in rank to Demetrius, and besides, he and Hermia are in love.) I am, my lord, as well-derived as he, as well-possessed. My love is more than his. And, which is more than all these boasts can be — I am beloved of beauteous Hermia! Why should not I then prosecute my right?

(The Duke sadly shakes his head to Lysander's plea, so the young man tells of Demetrius' past affair with another girl, who still worships him.) Demetrius made love to Nedar's daughter, Helena, and won her soul. And she, sweet lady, dotes, devoutly dotes, dotes in idolatry upon this spotted and inconstant man!

Theseus: (Worried, he admits he knows the gossip about Helena already.) I must confess that I have heard so much, and with Demetrius thought to have spoke thereof. *(He gestures towards the men.)* But, Demetrius, come. And come, Egeus. You shall go with me. *(He motions for them to enter the palace for a conference, adding a warning to Hermia to obey the laws.)* For you, fair

Hermia, look you arm yourself to fit your fancies to your father's will, or else the law of Athens yields you up — to death, or to a vow of single life!

(Turning to his bride) Come, my Hippolyta, *(But she is downcast, sad about the lovers.)* What cheer, my love! *(She tries to smile, and Theseus repeats his orders to the men.)* Demetrius and Egeus, go along. I must employ you in some business against our nuptial and confer with you of something that concerns yourselves.

Egeus: *(Bowing in obedience)* With duty and desire we follow you. *(Reluctantly he follows the Duke and Hippolyta, with a last threatening look at the lovers. Demetrius goes with him, proud and cold.)*

(Hermia and Lysander, left alone, rush into each other's arms. Lysander comforts her, brushing away her tears.)

Lysander: How now, my love! Why is your cheek so pale? *(He kisses her, trying to cheer her with reminders that other lovers have had problems too.)* Ay, me! For aught that I could ever read, the course of true love never did run smooth. *(Some lovers' families were not equal.)* But, either it was different in blood...

Hermia: *(With a sigh for the sweetheart too rich to wed a poorer love.)* O cross! Too high to be enthralled to low!

Lysander: *(Sometimes the lovers' ages did not match.)* Or else mis-grafted in respect of years...

Hermia: O spite! Too old to be engaged to young!

Lysander: (Sometimes the lovers had to let others arrange the marriage.) Or else it stood upon the choice of friends...

Hermia: O Hell! To choose love by another's eyes!

Lysander: (He sighs at still more problems for the perfect romance, making it short as a flash of lightning.) Or, if there were a sympathy in choice — war, death or sickness did lay siege to it, making it momentary as a sound, swift as a shadow, short as any dream, brief as the lightning in the night that unfolds both heaven and earth. And ere a man hath power to say, "Behold!" the jaws of darkness do devour it up. So quick bright things come to confusion.

Hermia: (Her shoulders sag with misery, as she sees Fate is sure to wreck all lovers' hopes. So they must be patient.) If then true lovers have been ever "crossed," it stands as an edict in destiny. Then let us teach our trial patience.

Lysander: (With a tone of reproach.) A good persuasion! *(His voice makes her look up, and he eagerly outlines a plan to make them free to marry.)* Therefore, hear me, Hermia. I have a widow aunt, a dowager of great revenue, and she hath no child. From Athens is her house remote — seven leagues! — and she respects me as her only son. There, gentle Hermia, may I marry thee! And to that place the sharp Athenian law cannot pursue us.

Lysander: If thou lovest me then, steal forth thy father's house tomorrow night.

If thou lovest me then, steal forth thy father's house tomorrow night. *(He recalls a wooded glen where they met once to gather May blossoms.)* And in the wood, a league without the town, where I did meet thee once with Helena to do observance to a morn of May, there will I stay for thee!

Hermia: (In joyous rapture, making all sorts of promises to run away and join him.) My good Lysander! I swear to thee, by Cupid's strongest bow, by his best arrow with the golden head, by the simplicity of Venus' doves, by all the vows that ever men have broke…*(She smiles in mischief.)* …in number more than ever women spoke, in that same place thou hast appointed me, tomorrow truly will I meet with thee!

Lysander: Keep promise, love! *(They are about to kiss when a tall blonde rushes in, Demetrius' former sweetheart, Helena.)* Look, here comes Helena!

Hermia: God speed, fair Helena! *(Wondering where Helena is running.)* Whither away?

Helena: (Stopping and bursting into tears, as if being called "fair" is a cruel joke.) Call you me "fair"? That "fair" again un-say. Demetrius loves your "fair." O happy fair!

(She looks at Hermia with envy, wishing all Hermia's charms were contagious, so Helena could attract Demetrius too.) Your eyes are lodestars, and your tongue's sweet air more tunable than lark to shepherd's ear, when wheat is green, when hawthorn buds appear. Sickness is catching — O, were favor so! Yours would I catch,

fair Hermia, ere I go. My ear should catch your voice, my eye your eye, my tongue should catch your tongue's sweet melody. O, teach me how you look, and with what art you sway the motion of Demetrius' heart!

Hermia: (Puzzled, for she tries to discourage Demetrius.) I frown upon him, yet he loves me still.

Helena: O, that your frowns would teach my smiles such skill!

Hermia: I give him curses, yet he gives me love.

Helena: O, that my prayers could such affection move!

Hermia: The more I hate, the more he follows me.

Helena: The more I love, the more he hateth me! *(She wipes her eyes.)*

Hermia: Take comfort. He no more shall see my face. *(In surprise, Helena stops in mid-cry and listens to the elopement plans.)* Lysander and myself will fly this place.

Lysander: Helen, to you our minds we will unfold. Tomorrow night, through Athens' gates have we devised to steal...

Hermia: ...and in the wood, where often you and I upon faint primrose beds were wont to lie, emptying our bosoms of their counsel sweet,... *(Helena nods, recalling their secret talking-place.)*...there my Lysander and myself shall meet. And thence from Athens turn away our eyes, to seek new friends and stranger companies.

(She kisses Helena, her dearest friend, goodbye.)
Farewell, sweet playfellow. Pray thou for us. And
good luck grant thee thy Demetrius!*(With a quick
kiss for Lysander, she leaves to prepare for their
journey.)*

Lysander: Helena, adieu. As you on him, Demetrius
dote on you! *(He leaves also. Helena, watching the
lovers go, speaks her thoughts aloud.)*

Helena: How happy some can be! *(She sighs and sits
on the staircase, chin in hand, brooding on her sad
romance and on Hermia's beauty.)* Through
Athens I am thought as fair as she. But what of
that? Demetrius thinks not so. Love looks not with
the eyes but with the mind, and therefore is
winged Cupid painted blind. For ere Demetrius
looked on Hermia's eyne, he hailed down oaths
that he was only mine!

*(Suddenly she realizes she has an excuse to see
Demetrius now — the elopement!)* I will go tell him
of fair Hermia's flight. Then to the wood will he
tomorrow night pursue her. And for this
intelligence, if I have thanks, it is a dear expense!
*(She rushes off to find Demetrius and thought-
lessly betray her friends, just for the chance to see
her love again.)*

Scene 2

*(In the House of Peter Quince, an elderly carpenter, a
number of handymen gather to rehearse a tragic play*

that Quince has written in honor of the Duke's wedding. The amateur actors include Quince, the would-be writer; stupid Snug, the joiner-carpenter; Flute, the squeaky-voiced bellows-mender; Snout, the practical tinker, a repairman for pots and pans; and Starveling, the timid tailor. But the chief actor is loud, enthusiastic Bottom, the weaver, who is so stage-struck that he wants to direct everything and to play all the parts too.)

Quince: Is all our company here?

Bottom: (In a big, jolly voice, giving advice for a roll call.) You were best to call them generally, man by man, according to the script.

Quince: (He takes out a long piece of paper and peers at it through his spectacles.) Here is the scroll of every man's name, which is thought fit, through all Athens, to play in our interlude before the Duke and the Duchess, on his wedding day at night.

Bottom: First, good Peter Quince, say what the play treats on. Then read the names of the actors, and so grow to a point.

Quince: (Announcing the title with pride.) Marry, our play is "The Most Lamentable Comedy and Most Cruel Death of Pyramus and Thisby."

Bottom: (Clapping his hands with enthusiasm.) A very good piece of work, I assure you, and a merry. Now, good Peter Quince, call forth your actors by the scroll. *(To the others, who are standing with mouths open at Quince's talent.)* Masters, spread yourselves. *(The workmen quickly sprawl on stools and on the floor.)*

Quince: Answer as I call you. Nick Bottom, the weaver!

Bottom: (Standing at attention) Ready! Name what
    part I am for, and proceed.

Quince: You, Nick Bottom, are set down for Pyramus.

Bottom: (Eagerly) What is Pyramus? A lover, or a
    tyrant?

Quince: A lover that kills himself, most gallant, for
    love!

*Bottom: (Striding up and down happily, he boasts of
    acting talent that can make the audience weep.)*
    That will ask some tears in the true performing of
    it. If I do it, let the audience look to their eyes. I will
    move storms! Yet…my chief humor is for a tyrant.
    *(He takes a pose like Hercules, glad to recite some
    very dignified bad poetry.)* I could play 'Ercles
    rarely, or a part to tear a cat in, to make all split…
    (He roars out words as he gestures grandly.)

    The raging rocks
    And shivering shocks
    Shall break the locks
      Of prison gates!
    (He waves towards the sun.)
    And Phibbus' car
    Shall shine from far,
    And make and mar
      The foolish Fates!

    *(He rubs his hands with satisfaction as the others
    burst into applause.)* This was lofty! *(To Quince)*
    Now name the rest of the players. *(To the others,*

he explains further.) This is 'Ercles' vein, a tyrant's vein. *(He speaks in a cooing voice.)* A lover is more...condoling. *(His soulful look breaks into a grin at their further applause.)*

Quince: (Peering at his list again.) Francis Flute, the bellows-mender.

Flute: (Squeaking) Here, Peter Quince!

Quince: Flute, you must take Thisby on you.

Flute: What is Thisby? *(He smiles brightly.)* A wandering knight?

Quince: It is the lady that Pyramus must love.

Flute: (His face falls, and he shrieks with horror.) Nay, faith, let not me play a woman! *(He rubs the few hairs on his chin.)* I have a beard coming!

Quince: (Not allowing any excuses) That's all one. You shall play it in a mask, and you may speak as small as you will.

Bottom: (Who wants to take every part.) An I may hide my face, let me play Thisby too. I'll speak in a monstrous little voice. *(In a bass voice, as Pyramus the lover, he calls out.)* "Thisne, Thisne!" *(To himself he cries an answer in a shrill woman's voice.)* "Ah, Pyramus, my lover dear! Thy Thisby dear, and lady dear!" *(He ends with a fluttering of eyelashes, as the listeners applaud again.)*

Quince: (Irritated) No, no! You must play Pyramus. And, Flute, you Thisby.

Bottom: (Disappointed) Well, proceed. *(He sits on a stool.)*

Bottom: Let me play the lion too! I will
roar, that I will make the Duke say,
"Let him roar again!"

Quince: Robin Starveling, the tailor!

Starveling: (Shyly) Here, Peter Quince.

Quince: Robin Starveling, you must play Thisby's mother...Tom Snout, the tinker!

Snout: (Solidly) Here, Peter Quince!

Quince: You, Pyramus' father...Myself, Thisby's father...Snug the joiner — you, the lion's part. *(He smiles at all broadly.)* And I hope here is a play fitted.

Snug: (Very dull-witted and slow to speak.) Have you the lion's part written? Pray you, if it be, give it me, for I am slow of study.

Quince: (Explaining it is ad lib.) You may do it extempore, for it is nothing but roaring.

Bottom: (With a leap to his feet in excitement.) Let me play the lion too! I will roar that I will do any man's heart good to hear me. *(He growls and roars mightily.)* I will roar, that I will make the Duke say, "Let him roar again! Let him roar again!"

Quince: (Looking over his spectacles with disapproval.) An you should do it too terribly, you would fright the Duchess and the ladies, and they would shriek. And that were enough to hang us all!

All: (Nodding in agreement, with the shadow of the gallows over them.) That would hang us, every mother's son!

Bottom: (Agreeing with the rest) I grant you, friends, if you should fright the ladies out of their wits, they

would have no more discretion but to hang us. *(He raises his voice melodiously.)* But I will aggravate my voice so that I will roar you as gently as any sucking dove. I will roar you, an 'twere any nightingale. *(He chirps out some little roars and smiles at the results.)*

Quince: (Firmly calming Bottom down with flattery.) You can play no part but Pyramus. For Pyramus is a sweet-faced man, a proper man as one shall see in a summer's day, a most lovely, gentleman-like man! Therefore you must needs play Pyramus.

Bottom: (Looking more handsome and heroic by the minute.) Well, I will undertake it. *(He struts about until a thought strikes him.)* What beard were I best to play it in?

Quince: (Shrugging) Why, what you will.

Bottom: (Listing his wardrobe of beards.) I will discharge it in either your straw-color beard, your orange-tawny beard, your purple-in-grain beard, or your French-crown-color beard, your perfect yellow.

Quince: (With absolute authority) You will play bare-faced. *(Bottom gasps in disappointment, but Quince distracts him by giving out various scrolls.)* But, masters, here are your parts. And I am to entreat you, request you, and desire you to con them by tomorrow night. *(All begin to check to see how many lines they have to learn.)* And meet me in the palace wood, a mile without the town, by moonlight. There we will rehearse. For if we meet in the city, we shall be dogged with company, and our devices known. *(He begins a list of stage equipment needed.)* In the meantime I will draw a bill of properties, such as our play wants. I pray you, fail me not!

Bottom: *(With loud approval, he agrees in the largest words he thinks he knows the meaning of.)* We will meet. And there we may rehearse most obscenely and courageously! *(With warnings to the other actors.)* Take pains! Be perfect! Adieu!

Quince: At the Duke's Oak we meet.

Bottom: Enough! *(He shakes hands in agreement with the others, using an archer's word of promise.)* Hold, or cut bowstrings! *(They leave to study their parts before the rehearsal in the wood.)*

ACT II

Scene 1

(In the wood near Athens the next evening, moonlight floods the scene of great old oaks overhanging little meadows filled with flowers. A tiny winged fairy enters from one side, sprinkling dewdrops around the orbit of a mushroom ring on the grass. From the other side comes Puck, also called Robin Goodfellow, a cheerful hobgoblin who looks like a naughty little boy with pointed ears.)

Puck: How now, spirit! Whither wander you?

Fairy: (Singing as she dances about.)
>   Over hill, over dale,
>   Thorough bush, thorough brier,
>   Over park, over pale,
>   Thorough flood, thorough fire,
>   I do wander everywhere,
>   Swifter than the moon's sphere.
>   And I serve the Fairy Queen,
>   To dew her orbs upon the green.
>   I must go seek some dewdrops here,
>   And hang a pearl in every cowslip's ear.

>   Farewell, thou lob of spirits. I'll be gone. *(Pointing to the mushroom ring, where the Fairy Queen Titania soon will dance.)* Our Queen and all her elves come here anon!

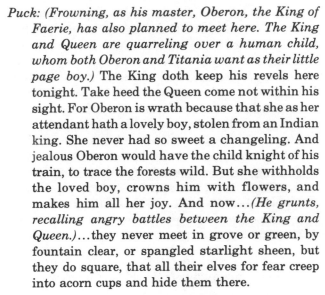

Puck: (Frowning, as his master, Oberon, the King of Faerie, has also planned to meet here. The King and Queen are quarreling over a human child, whom both Oberon and Titania want as their little page boy.) The King doth keep his revels here tonight. Take heed the Queen come not within his sight. For Oberon is wrath because that she as her attendant hath a lovely boy, stolen from an Indian king. She never had so sweet a changeling. And jealous Oberon would have the child knight of his train, to trace the forests wild. But she withholds the loved boy, crowns him with flowers, and makes him all her joy. And now...*(He grunts, recalling angry battles between the King and Queen.)*...they never meet in grove or green, by fountain clear, or spangled starlight sheen, but they do square, that all their elves for fear creep into acorn cups and hide them there.

Fairy: (Looking at Puck closely, for she has heard of Puck's naughty tricks.) Either I mistake your shape and making quite, or else you are that shrewd and knavish sprite called Robin Goodfellow. Are not you he that frights the maidens of the villagery? And sometime mislead night wanderers, laughing at their harm? *(Puck laughs gleefully and nods, while the Fairy tells of his doing chores for friends also.)* Those that "Hobgoblin" call you, and "Sweet Puck," you do their work, and they shall have good luck. Are not you he?

Puck: Thou speakest aright. I am that merry wanderer of the night. *(He recounts other tricks —*

misleading a horse by looking like a young mare.)
I jest to Oberon and make him smile, when I a fat
and bean-fed horse beguile, neighing in likeness of
a filly foal. *(At times he pretends to be a floating
crabapple so an old woman spills her drink.)* And
sometime lurk I in a gossip's bowl in very likeness
of a roasted crab; and when she drinks, against
her lips I bob, and on her withered dewlap pour the
ale. *(He may imitate a stool and make a storyteller
fall on the floor.)* The wisest aunt, telling the
saddest tale, sometime for three-foot stool
mistaketh me. Then slip I from her bum! Down
topples she! *(He looks into the shadows and perks
up his pointed ears.)* But, room, Fairy! Here comes
Oberon!

Fairy: (Looking the other way, into the moonlight.)
And here my mistress! Would that he were gone!

*(The King and Queen of Fairies enter with their
attendants. Both are beautifully dressed in fan-
tastic costumes. Oberon has black horns and dark
double wings, while Titania wears a lovely long
cobweb gown, glittering jewels in her hair, and
large fragile wings. Beside Titania is the little
Indian child dressed in turban and brocaded suit.
As the two Royal fairies meet, their tempers flare.)*

Oberon: Ill met by moonlight, proud Titania!

Titania: What, jealous Oberon! *(To the Dewdrop Fairy)*
Fairy, skip hence. I have forsworn his bed and
company. *(Titania also turns to go, but Oberon
holds her fast by her wing.)*

Oberon: Ill met by moonlight, proud Titania!

Oberon: Tarry, rash wanton! Am I not thy lord?

Titania: Then I must be thy lady. But I know when thou hast stolen away from Fairy Land. *(She is sure he has returned only to wish luck to Hippolyta, his former love, who will marry Duke Theseus.)* Why art thou here, come from the farthest steep of India? But that, forsooth, the bouncing Amazon, your warrior love, to Theseus must be wedded, and you come to give their bed joy and prosperity.

Oberon: (In answer, he accuses her of having had an affair with the Duke.) How canst thou thus for shame, Titania, glance at my credit with Hippolyta, knowing I know thy love to Theseus?

Titania: (Denying everything except his constant interruption of her fairies' dances.) These are the forgeries of jealousy. And never, since the middle summer's spring, met we on hill, in dale, forest, or mead, by paved fountain or by rushy brook, or in the beached margent of the sea, to dance our ringlets to the whistling wind, but with thy brawls thou has disturbed our sport.

Oberon: (Trying to make peace) Why should Titania cross her Oberon? I do but beg a little changeling boy, to be my henchman.

Titania: (She clasps the Indian child to her, for the child's mother was a friend and follower of Titania's before she died.) Set your heart at rest. The Fairy Land buys not the child of me. His mother was a votress of my order, and, in the

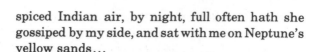

spiced Indian air, by night, full often hath she gossiped by my side, and sat with me on Neptune's yellow sands...

(She smiles to remember how they watched great merchant ships, which the pregnant mother imitated as she walked, bringing Titania little gifts.)...marking the embarked traders on the flood, when we have laughed to see the sails conceive and grow big-bellied with the wanton wind; which she, with pretty and with swimming gait following — her womb then rich with my young squire — would imitate, and sail upon the land to fetch me trifles, and return again, as from a voyage, rich with merchandise.

(Sadly) But she, being mortal, of that boy did die. And for her sake do I rear up her boy, and for her sake I will not part with him!

Oberon: *(Coldly ignoring her claim to the child.)* How long within this wood intend you stay?

Titania: Perchance till after Theseus' wedding day. *(She invites him to join her group or to ignore them.)* If you will patiently dance in our round and see our moonlight revels, go with us. If not, shun me, and I will spare your haunts.

Oberon: Give me that boy, and I will go with thee!

Titania: Not for thy fairy kingdom! *(To her followers)* Fairies, away! *(They gather about the little Indian boy, and all fly off with him.)*

Oberon: *(As he looks after his Queen, he swears revenge.)* Well, go thy way. Thou shalt not from this grove till I torment thee for this injury. *(To his little goblin)* My gentle Puck, come hither. *(He recalls to Puck a cliff where he heard a mermaid's song that smoothed the sea and made the stars to fall.)* Thou rememberest since once I sat upon a promontory, and heard a mermaid, on a dolphin's back, uttering such dulcet and harmonious breath that the rude sea grew civil at her song, and certain stars shot madly from their spheres, to hear the sea maid's music?

Puck: I remember.

Oberon: That very time I saw — but thou couldst not — flying between the cold moon and the earth, Cupid all armed. *(He recalls how Cupid shot a love-arrow at a virgin queen, Elizabeth, but it missed its mark and hit a little flower, turning it into an herb of love.)* A certain aim he took at a fair vestal throned by the west, and loosed his love-shaft smartly from his bow. But the imperial votress passed on in maiden meditation, fancy-free. Yet marked I where the bolt of Cupid fell. It fell upon a little western flower — before milk-white, now purple with love's wound — and maidens call it "love-in-idleness." Fetch me that flower. The herb I showed thee once.

(He whispers into Puck's pointed ear the mystic secret: the flower-juice tricks a sleeper into falling in love with the next thing it spies.) The juice of it on sleeping eyelids laid will make or man or woman madly dote upon the next live creature that it sees! *(Puck spreads his big mouth in a grin.)* Fetch me this herb, and be thou here again!

Puck: (Ready to circle the world in a flash.) I'll put a girdle round about the earth in forty minutes! *(He races off.)*

Oberon: (With satisfaction he speaks his thoughts aloud.) Having once this juice, I'll watch Titania when she is asleep, and drop the liquor of it in her eyes. The next thing then she waking looks upon — be it on lion, bear, or wolf, or bull, on meddling monkey, or on busy ape — she shall pursue it with the soul of love!

(Before giving her the antidote, he plans to steal the Indian child.) And ere I take this charm from off her sight, as I can take it with another herb, I'll make her render up her page to me. *(A noise distracts him.)* But who comes here? *(He wraps his cloak of darkness about him and prepares to spy on the intruders.)* I am invisible, and I will overhear their conference.

(Demetrius enters, looking about for the eloping lovers, Hermia and Lysander. He shouts in irritation at Helena, who stumbles along after him, her long blonde hair tangled by the bushes.)

Demetrius: I love thee not. Therefore pursue me not. Where is Lysander and fair Hermia? *(He draws his sword.)* The one I'll slay. *(He puts his other hand to his love-wounded heart.)* The other slayeth me. *(To Helena)* Thou toldst me they were stolen unto this wood, and here am I. *(She comes to lean on his shoulder, and he pushes her away.)* Hence, get thee gone, and follow me no more!

Helena: (Magnetized) You draw me, you hard-hearted adamant!

Demetrius: (Mocking her with questions) Do I entice you? Do I speak you fair? Or, rather, do I not in plainest truth tell you — I do not nor I cannot love you?

Helena: And even for that do I love you the more! *(Kneeling at his feet, she whimpers.)* I am your spaniel. Spurn me, strike me, neglect me, lose me! Only give me leave, unworthy as I am, to follow you!

Demetrius: (He kicks at her.) I am sick when I do look on thee!

Helena: And I am sick when I look not on you.

Demetrius: (With a harsh warning) I'll run from thee and hide me, and leave thee to the mercy of wild beasts.

Helena: The wildest hath not such a heart as you! *(She clings to him.)*

Demetrius: (Shaking her off and drawing his sword to threaten her.) Let me go! Or, if thou follow me, do not believe but I shall do thee mischief in the wood!

Helena: Ay, in the Temple, in the town, the field, you do me mischief! *(She puts her hand to her aching heart.)* Fie, Demetrius! *(But he runs off, his sword in hand. She cries out after him.)* I'll follow thee, and make a Heaven of Hell, to die upon the hand I love so well. *(And she stumbles after him, calling his name.)*

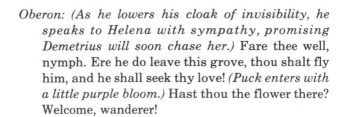

Oberon: (As he lowers his cloak of invisibility, he speaks to Helena with sympathy, promising Demetrius will soon chase her.) Fare thee well, nymph. Ere he do leave this grove, thou shalt fly him, and he shall seek thy love! *(Puck enters with a little purple bloom.)* Hast thou the flower there? Welcome, wanderer!

Puck: Ay, there it is. *(He waves the magic flower in the air.)*

Oberon: I pray thee, give it me. *(Puck hands Oberon the little flower and sits while Oberon describes Titania's garden bower, where he will trick her when asleep.)* I know a bank where the wild thyme blows, where oxlips and the nodding violet grows, quite over-canopied with luscious woodbine, with sweet musk roses, and with eglantine. There sleeps Titania sometime of the night, lulled in these flowers with dances and delight. And there the snake throws her enameled skin wide enough to wrap a fairy in. *(He looks at the magic flower.)* And with the juice of this, I'll streak her eyes and make her full of hateful fantasies.

(Puck giggles. Oberon quiets him, and he gives him half the flower as he points after Helena and Demetrius.) Take thou some of it, and seek through this grove. A sweet Athenian lady is in love with a disdainful youth. Anoint his eyes. *(Puck nods vigorously.)* But do it when the next thing he espies may be the lady. *(The elf grins with understanding.)* Thou shalt know the man by the Athenian garments he hath on. And look thou meet me ere the first cock crow!

Puck: Fear not, my lord. Your servant shall do so!

   (They fly off in different directions, Oberon to charm Titania, and Puck to charm the unknown young man from Athens.)

Scene 2

(In another part of the wood, Titania enters with her followers and the little Indian child. In the background is her bower of flowers and greenery, where she sleeps. A bank of wild thyme, honeysuckle and roses, a hawthorn hedge, and a little meadow complete the scene. Titania claps her hands, and the others listen as she tells them to sing and dance before they leave for work — to protect roses, make war with bats called "reremice," and keep away the owls — while she rests in the bower.)

Titania: Come, now a roundel and a fairy song. Then, for the third part of a minute, hence — some to kill cankers in the musk-rose buds, some war with reremice for their leathern wings to make my small elves coats, and some keep back the clamorous owl, that nightly hoots and wonders at our quaint spirits. Sing me now asleep. Then to your offices, and let me rest. *(The Fairies sing as they dance in a circle. Titania watches them from her bed of flowers, sheltered from dew by the bower composed of branches like a little tent.)*

1st Fairy:

> You spotted snakes with double tongue,
>> Thorny hedgehogs, be not seen.
> Newts and blindworms, do no wrong —
>> Come not near our Fairy Queen.

Chorus: (Urging the nightingale, Philomele, to sing to the Queen.)

> Philomele, with melody
>> Sing in our sweet lullaby.
> Lulla, lulla, lullaby, lulla, lulla, lullaby.
>> Never harm
>> Nor spell nor charm,
> Come our lovely lady nigh.
> So, good night, with lullaby.

1st Fairy:

> Weaving spiders, come not here.
>> Hence, you long-legged spinners, hence!
> Beetles black, approach not near.
>> Worm nor snail, do no offense!

Chorus: Philomele, with melody, etc.

2nd Fairy: (To the others, in a chant.)

> Hence, away! Now all is well.
> One aloof stand sentinel!

(The Fairies disappear, and Titania sinks into sleep, her elf-guard far off. With his cloak of invisibility drawn around him, Oberon enters and looks about. Titania moves and murmurs in her sleep. Certain he is not seen, he tiptoes to her and squeezes the flower over Titania's eyelids, to charm her into falling madly in love with the next living thing she sees, even an ounce or lynx, or "pard," short for leopard.)

Oberon:

> What thou seest when thou dost wake,
> Do it for thy true-love take!
> Love and languish for his sake.
> Be it ounce, or cat, or bear,
> Pard, or boar with bristled hair,
> In thy eye that shall appear,
> When thou wakest, it is thy dear.
> Wake when some vile thing is near!

(He flies away, and for a moment Titania sleeps on the flowers in the moonlight, alone in the woodland scene. But the lovers Hermia and Lysander enter, lost in the wood on their way to his rich aunt's house. They droop with weariness as he helps her to the fragrant slope of wild thyme.)

Lysander: Fair love, you faint with wandering in the wood. And to speak truth, I have forgot our way. We'll rest us, Hermia, if you think it good, and tarry for the comfort of the day.

Hermia: (Lying down on the herb-bed.) Be it so, Lysander. Find you out a bed, for I upon this bank will rest my head.

Lysander: (Sinking down beside her and taking her in his arms.) One turf shall serve as pillow for us both — one heart, one bed, two bosoms, and one troth.

Hermia: (Modestly startled) Nay, good Lysander. For my sake, my dear, lie further off yet. Do not lie so near. *(To sleep far apart is much more suitable.)* Such separation as may well be said becomes a virtuous bachelor and a maid. So far be distant.

And good night, sweet friend. *(They kiss, and she prays their love will not change until death.)* Thy love ne'er alter till thy sweet life end!

Lysander: Amen, amen to that fair prayer, say I. And then end life when I end loyalty! *(So swearing his love, he moves away and lies down.)* Here is my bed.

(The exhausted lovers fall asleep almost instantly. After a moment, Puck enters, the love-flower in his hand, still searching for the cold Athenian lover with his heartsick maiden whom Oberon saw.)

Puck:
Through the forest have I gone,
But Athenian found I none.
Night and silence…Who is here?
(He inspects Lysander's clothes.)
Weeds of Athens he doth wear.
This is he, my master said,
Despised the Athenian maid.
(He spies Hermia and tiptoes to her.)
And here the maiden, sleeping sound
On the dank and dirty ground.

(Completely mistaken — for he believes the couple are Demetrius and Helena — he thinks Lysander has rejected Hermia's love because they sleep modestly apart.)

Pretty soul! She durst not lie
Near this lack-love, this kill-courtesy.
(Going to Lysander, he calls him a crude name as he squeezes the magic juice on his eyes.)

Puck:
  Churl, upon thy eyes I throw
  All the power this charm doth owe.

Churl, upon thy eyes I throw
All the power this charm doth owe.
When thou wakest, let love forbid
Sleep his seat on thy eyelid.
So awake when I am gone,
For I must now to Oberon!
*(He scampers off to his master, not seeing
Demetrius enter, with Helena running after him.)*

Helena: *(Trying to stop him.)* Stay, though thou kill
me, sweet Demetrius!

Demetrius: *(Pushing her, so she falls on the ground.)*
I charge thee, hence, and do not haunt me thus!
(He prepares to run away.)

Helena: *(Frightened of the forest gloom.)* O, wilt thou
darkling leave me? Do not so!

Demetrius: Stay, on thy peril! I alone will go. *(He runs
off. Helena, not seeing her sleeping friends, leans
on a fallen log and cries.)*

Helena: O, I am out of breath in this fond chase! The
more my prayer, the lesser is my grace. *(With envy
for Hermia)* Happy is Hermia, wheresoe'er she
lies, for she hath blessed and attractive eyes. How
came her eyes so bright? Not with salt tears. If so,
my eyes are oftener washed than hers. No, no, I
am as ugly as a bear, for beasts that meet me run
away for fear.

*(She glances about as a moonbeam strikes
Lysander, and she rises and runs to him.)* But who
is here? Lysander! On the ground! Dead? Or
asleep? I see no blood, no wound. *(Shaking his
shoulder)* Lysander, if you live, good sir, awake!

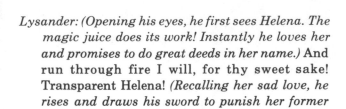

Lysander: (Opening his eyes, he first sees Helena. The magic juice does its work! Instantly he loves her and promises to do great deeds in her name.) And run through fire I will, for thy sweet sake! Transparent Helena! *(Recalling her sad love, he rises and draws his sword to punish her former sweetheart.)* Where is Demetrius? O, how fit a word is that vile name to perish on my sword!

Helena: (With alarm) Do not say so, Lysander, say not so! What though he love your Hermia? Lord, what though? Yet Hermia still loves you. Then be content.

Lysander: (Rejecting Hermia and the time he wasted with her.) Content with Hermia? No! I do repent the tedious minutes I with her have spent. *(Falling on his knees in worship of Helena.)* Not Hermia but **Helena** I love! Who will not change a raven for a dove?

Helena: (Backing away, as she thinks he is making fun of her.) Wherefore was I to this keen mockery born? When at your hands did I deserve this scorn? But fare you well. *(She sadly scolds him, for she thought he had kinder manners.)* Perforce, I must confess I thought you lord of more true gentleness. *(To herself, as she runs away, crying.)* O, that a lady of one man refused, should of another therefore be abused!

Lysander: (Looking after her) She sees not Hermia. *(To his sleeping sweetheart, as if she were a loathsome monster.)* Hermia, sleep thou there, and never mayst thou come Lysander near! Thou of all be hated! *(Looking again after Helena)* And, all my powers, address your love and might to honor Helen and to be her knight! *(He runs off after his new love.)*

Hermia: (After moving and crying in the grip of a nightmare, she calls out, pulling an imaginary snake from her body.) Help me, Lysander! Help me! Do thy best to pluck this crawling serpent from my breast! *(Sitting up, she looks about in sleepy relief.)* Ay me, for pity! What a dream was here! *(She lifts a shaking hand and gazes at it.)* Lysander, look how I do quake with fear. Methought a serpent eat my heart away, and you sat smiling at his cruel prey.

(She laughs at the stupid dream, but no Lysander answers her. Her laughter dies, and she calls out again.) Lysander! *(She sees his empty sleeping place.)* What, removed? Lysander! *(No answer comes, and she becomes increasingly uneasy.)* Lord! What, out of hearing? Gone? No sound, no word? Alack, where are you? *(Silence is the only answer.)* No? Then I well perceive you are not nigh. *(Rising, she looks about, frightened.)* Either death or you I'll find immediately! *(She leaves to search for him.)*

(Titania slumbers alone in the wood on her flower-bed, the love-juice on her eyes, prepared to make her fall in love also with the next creature she sees.)

ACT III

Scene 1

(The same scene continues. From the hawthorn hedge or brake come the slow-witted workers from Athens to rehearse their play. Not noticing the sleeping Fairy Queen, Peter Quince leads the others into the grassy clearing, where the hawthorn screen will make a good dressing room.)

Bottom: Are we all met? *(He clutches his script with excitement.)*

Quince: (Clapping his hands in satisfaction.) Pat, pat! *(He glances about.)* And here's a marvelous convenient place for our rehearsal. This green plot shall be our stage, this hawthorn brake our tiring house, and...we will do it "in action," as we will do it before the Duke!

Bottom: (Unfolding his script with a worried air.) Peter Quince?

Quince: What sayest thou, bully Bottom?

Bottom: (Pointing to the end of the scroll.) There are things in this comedy of Pyramus and Thisby that will never please. First, Pyramus must draw a sword to kill himself, which the ladies cannot abide. How answer you that?

Snout: (Nodding agreement that it is perilous.) By our ladykin, a par'lous fear!

Starveling: I believe we must leave the killing out, when all is done.

Bottom: (Trying to hide his overwhelming desire to be playwright and director too.) Not a whit. I have a device to make all well. *(Quince raises an eyebrow in question, as Bottom explains to him.)* Write me a prologue, and let the prologue seem to say we will do no harm with our swords, and that Pyramus is not killed indeed. And, for the more better assurance, tell them that I, Pyramus, am not Pyramus but Bottom the weaver. This will put them out of fear.

Quince: (Adjusting his spectacles) Well, we will have such a prologue. *(He makes a note of it on the stack of papers he carries.)*

Snout: (Timidly) Will not the ladies be afeared of the lion?

Starveling: I fear it, I promise you. *(Everyone appears uneasy.)*

Bottom: (With a whisper of horror.) Masters, you ought to consider with yourselves: to bring in — God shield us! — a **lion** among ladies is a most dreadful thing! For there is not a more fearful wild fowl than your lion living. And we ought to look to it! *(The others nod their heads in terrified agreement.)*

Snout: Therefore, another prologue must tell he is not a lion. *(He smiles.)*

Bottom: (Improving the idea) Nay, you must name his name, and half his face must be seen through the lion's neck. *(The others cheer with relief, and Bottom continues, imitating how the lion should talk through the hole beneath the mask.)* And he himself must speak through, saying thus, or to the same defect: "Ladies,"...or, "Fair ladies, I would wish you,"...or, "I would request you,"...or, "I would entreat you not to fear, not to tremble. If you think I come hither as a lion...no, I am no such thing. I am a man as other men are." And there indeed let him name his name, and tell them plainly he is Snug the joiner.

Quince: Well, it shall be so. *(He jots down notes and stops, puzzled about other production problems.)* But there is two hard things: that is, to bring the moonlight into a chamber. For, you know, Pyramus and Thisby meet by moonlight.

Snout: Doth the moon shine that night we play our play?

Bottom: A calendar, a calendar! Look in the almanac. Find out moonshine, find out moonshine!

Quince: (He searches through his papers and brings out an almanac.) Yes, it doth shine that night.

Bottom: Why, then may you leave a casement of the great chamber window, where we play, open, and the moon may shine in at the casement!

Quince: Ay. *(Thinking of the legend of the Man in the Moon who gathers firewood on Sunday with his dog.)* Or else one must come in with a bush of thorns and a lantern, and say he comes to disfigure, or to present, the person of Moonshine. *(They all agree heartily.)* Then, there is another thing: we must have a wall in the great chamber. For Pyramus and Thisby, says the story, did talk through the chink of a wall.

Snout: *(Scratching his sensible head)* You can never bring in a wall. What say you, Bottom?

Bottom: *(Always with a ready suggestion.)* Some man or other must present Wall. And let him have some plaster, or some loam, or some rough-cast about him, to signify Wall. And let him hold his fingers thus...*(He puts out his hand with two fingers held wide apart.)*...and through that cranny shall Pyramus and Thisby whisper!

Quince: *(Smiling)* If that may be, then all is well. *(The rest murmur agreement, and Quince starts the actual business of the rehearsal.)* Come, sit down, every mother's son, and rehearse your parts. Pyramus, you begin. When you have spoken your speech, enter into that brake. *(He points to the hawthorn hedge.)* And so everyone according to his cue.

(They sit, still not noticing the sleeping Titania. Bottom goes to the center of the "stage," takes a deep breath and poses like a hero. At this moment, little Puck peeps out from behind the hawthorn brake in amazement.)

Puck: *(To himself)* What hempen homespuns have we swaggering here, so near the cradle of the Fairy Queen? *(He sees the scripts.)* What, a play toward? I'll be an auditor — an actor too perhaps, if I see cause!

Quince: Speak, Pyramus! Thisby, stand forth. *(Flute comes forward unhappily. He drags his feet, as he tries to look like a sweet young girl in spite of being six feet tall with whiskers. Bottom takes him by the hand, making Flute blush and wiggle with embarrassment.)*

Bottom: Thisby, the flowers of odious savors sweet...

Quince: (Correcting him) Odors, odors!

Bottom: ...odors savors sweet: so hath thy breath, my dearest Thisby dear. *(He holds his hand to his ear and listens.)* But hark, a voice! Stay thou but here awhile, and by and by I will to thee appear. *(He exits to the hawthorn brake.)*

Flute: Must I speak now?

Quince: Ay, marry, must you. For you must understand he goes but to see a noise that he heard, and is to come again.

Flute: (Reciting his lines in a high girlish voice, he says them so fast, jumbled together, that they hardly make sense.) Most radiant Pyramus, most lily-white of hue, of color like the red rose on triumphant brier, most brisky juvenal, and eke most lovely Jew, as true as truest horse, that yet would never tire, I'll meet thee, Pyramus, at Ninny's tomb!

Quince: (Like a director) "Ninus' tomb," man! Why, you must not speak that yet. That you answer to Pyramus. You speak all your part at once, cues and all. *(Calls out)* Pyramus, enter! Your cue is past. It is "never tire."

Flute: (Repeating) O…as true as truest horse, that yet would never tire. *(From behind the hawthorn come Bottom and Puck, who is doubled over from laughter. He has changed Bottom's head to a donkey's head. Bottom, however, does not know his head has been changed, and he says his correct lines to Flute.)*

Bottom: If I were fair, Thisby, I were only thine!

(For a moment, the actors freeze in horror, looking at the long ears and hairy snout on Bottom, Bottom stares back and blinks his big eyes. Then the others race about in terror, falling over one another, to escape such witchcraft.)

Quince: O monstrous! O strange! We are haunted. Pray, masters…Fly, masters! Help! *(All the craftsmen run off, leaving Bottom puzzled. He scratches his hairy ears in wonder. Puck dances about with glee, shouting after the stupid clowns.)*

Puck: I'll follow you, I'll lead you about a round, through bog, through bush, through brake, through brier. Sometime a horse I'll be, sometime a hound, a hog, a headless bear, sometime a fire. And neigh and bark and grunt, and roar and burn, like horse, hound, hog, bear, fire, at every turn. *(He scampers off to tease the handymen further.)*

Bottom: (Shaking his furry head) Why do they run away? This is a knavery of them to make me afeard.

Snout: (Entering with caution to make sure he has seen correctly.) O Bottom, thou art changed! What do I see on thee?

Bottom: (In anger, he shakes his fist at him.) What do
you see? You see an ass-head of your own, do you?
(Snout runs away.)

*Quince: (Enters, crossing his fingers to ward off evil
enchantments.)* Bless thee, Bottom! Bless thee!
Thou art translated! *(He runs off also.)*

*Bottom: (Sure that his friends are playing a trick on
him.)* I see their knavery. This is to make an ass of
me — to fright me, if they could. But I will not stir
from this place, do what they can! I will walk up
and down here, and will sing, that they shall hear
I am not afraid. *(As he sings and talks, his voice
becomes more of a donkey's bray, and occasion-
ally he goes "Hee-haw!" without noticing it. He
begins an old folk song about birds.)*
The woosel cock so black of hue,
    With orange-tawny bill,
The throstle with his note so true,
    The wren with little quill...

*Titania: (Awakening at the loud singing, she sees
Bottom. Instantly the magic juice does its work,
and she is in love with him, donkey-head and all.)*
What angel wakes me from my flowery bed?

Bottom: (Still singing)
The finch, the sparrow, and the lark,
    The plain-song cuckoo gray,
Whose note full many a man doth mark,
    And dares not answer nay....
*(He stops to pick a bunch of grass and eat it.
Titania comes forward, her wings fluttering with
love. She puts her beautiful arms around Bottom
and kisses his hairy cheeks.)*

Titania: I pray thee, gentle mortal, sing again! *(She strokes his head, and his long ears wig-wag back and forth with surprise, though he tries to be cool and nonchalant.)* Mine ear is much enamored of thy note. So is mine eye enthralled to thy shape, on the first view, to say...to swear, I love thee!

Bottom: Methinks, mistress, you should have little reason for that. *(She continues to kiss him, and he shrugs at her lack of sense.)* And yet, to say the truth, reason and love keep little company together nowadays!

Titania: (In a voice like a cooing dove.) Thou art as wise as thou art beautiful.

Bottom: Not so, neither. *(Looking about for an escape.)* But if I had wit enough to get out of this wood, I have enough to serve mine own turn.

Titania: (Holding on to him) Out of this wood do not desire to go. Thou shalt remain here, whether thou wilt or no. *(He stops his attempt to leave as she continues.)* I am a spirit of no common rate, and I do love thee. Therefore, go with me. I'll give thee fairies to attend on thee, and they shall fetch thee jewels from the deep, and sing, while thou on pressed flowers dost sleep. *(With a last shrug of defeat, he turns to her and embraces her, as if deciding to enjoy this strange development. She pats his muzzle, and his upper lip curls with pleasure. Daintily, she calls her attendants.)* Peaseblossom! Cobweb! Moth! And Mustardseed! *(The four Fairies enter instantly.)*

Peaseblossom: Ready!

Cobweb: And I!

Moth: And I!

Mustardseed: And I!

All: Where shall we go?

Titania: (With her arms about Bottom, who assumes kingly airs, she tells the fairies ways to entertain her new love.) Be kind and courteous to this gentleman. Hop in his walks, and gambol in his eyes. Feed him with apricocks and dewberries, with purple grapes, green figs, and mulberries. *(From bees they are to get honey and beeswax for candles.)* The honey bags steal from the humble-bees. And for night tapers, crop their waxen thighs and light them at the fiery glowworm's eyes, to have my love to bed and to arise. And pluck the wings from painted butterflies, to fan the moonbeams from his sleeping eyes. Nod to him, elves, and do him courtesies!

Peaseblossom: (Making a curtsey to the ground.) Hail, mortal!

Cobweb: Hail!

Moth: Hail!

Mustardseed: Hail!

Bottom: (Bowing to them in return.) I cry your worships mercy, heartily. *(To Cobweb)* I beseech your worship's name.

Cobweb: Cobweb.

Titania: Tie up my love's tongue. Bring him silently!

Bottom: I shall desire you of more acquaintance, good Master Cobweb. *(He helps himself to a strand of web from the fairy's tunic and pretends to wind it like a bandage around his thumb as if to stop some bleeding.)* If I cut my finger, I shall make bold with you. *(To the next Fairy)* Your name, honest gentleman?

Peaseblossom: Peaseblossom.

Bottom: I pray you, commend me to Mistress Squash, your mother, and to Master Peascod, your father. Good Master Peaseblossom, I shall desire you of more acquaintance too. *(To the next)* Your name, I beseech you, sir?

Mustardseed: Mustardseed.

Bottom: Good Master Mustardseed! *(He fans his open mouth as if his tongue is burnt from the spice.)* I promise you, your kindred hath made my eyes water ere now. I desire you of more acquaintance, good Master Mustardseed. *(All bow to each other graciously.)*

Titania: (To all the Fairies) Come, wait upon him. Lead him to my bower. *(Looking above at the dewy moonlight.)* The moon, methinks, looks with a watery eye. And when she weeps, weeps every little flower, lamenting some enforced chastity. Tie up my love's tongue. Bring him silently!

(The Fairies weave ropes and garlands of flowers around Bottom, who allows himself to be led to the Fairy Queen's bed of flowers. There she folds him in her arms and snuggles down beside him. His

*big donkey-eyes blink at this strange situation,
and one ear gives a little twitch of astonishment.)*

Scene 2

*(In another part of the wood, Oberon, the Fairy King,
waits to hear the news of the magic flower-juice from
Puck.)*

Oberon: I wonder if Titania be awaked. Then, what
it was that next came in her eye, which she must
dote on in extremity. *(Puck enters, laughing
heartily.)* Here comes my messenger. How now,
mad spirit?

Puck: (Pointing behind him) My mistress with a
monster is in love! *(Oberon gestures for him to tell
more.)* Near to her close and consecrated bower,
while she was in her dull and sleeping hour, a crew
of patches — rude mechanicals that work for
bread upon Athenian stalls — were met together to
rehearse a play, intended for great Theseus'
nuptial day.

(He describes Bottom.) The shallowest thick-skin
of that barren sort, who Pyramus presented in
their sport, forsook his scene, and entered in a
brake. When I did him at this advantage take, an
ass's nole I fixed on his head. Anon his Thisby
must be answered, and forth my mimic comes.
*(Oberon smiles, and Puck acts out the earlier scene
to illustrate his story.)* When they him spy, so, at

his sight, away his fellows fly! I led them on in
this distracted fear, and left "sweet Pyramus"
translated there. *(Laughing again at the silly
results of the magic.)* When, in that moment, so it
came to pass, Titania waked, and straightway
loved an ass!

Oberon: *(Amused)* This falls out better than I could
devise. *(He remembers the other orders he gave
Puck.)* But hast thou yet latched the Athenian's
eyes with the love juice, as I did bid thee do?

Puck: I took him sleeping. That is finished too. And
the Athenian woman by his side, that, when he
waked, of force she must be eyed.

*(Hermia enters, looking desperately for Lysander.
And following her is Demetrius, still demanding
that she marry him.)*

Oberon: *(To Puck, as he folds them both in his cloak
of invisibility.)* Stand close. This is the same
Athenian.

Puck: *(Puzzled)* This is the woman, but not this the
man.

Demetrius: *(To Hermia)* O, why rebuke you him that
loves you so?

Hermia: *(Believing Demetrius is responsible for
Lysander's absence.)* If thou hast slain Lysander
in his sleep, kill me too. Would he have stolen away
from sleeping Hermia? It cannot be but thou hast
murdered him. *(She stares at his serious face.)* So
should a murderer look, so dead, so grim.

Demetrius: (With reproach) So should the **murdered** look. And so should I, pierced through the heart with your stern cruelty.

Hermia: What's this to my Lysander? Where is he? Ah, good Demetrius, wilt thou give him me? *(Her love for Lysander is like a slap to Demetrius.)*

Demetrius: I had rather give his carcass to my hounds!

Hermia: (In a burst of temper.) Out, dog! Out, cur! Has thou slain him then?

Demetrius: (Sulkily) I am not guilty of Lysander's blood. Nor is he dead, for aught that I can tell.

Hermia: (Pleading) I pray thee, tell me then that he is well.

Demetrius: And if I could, what should I get therefore? *(He tries to kiss her.)*

Hermia: (Pushing him away) A privilege, never to see me more! *(She starts to leave)* And from thy hated presence part I so. See me no more, whether he be dead or no. *(She runs off, and Demetrius gives up trying to follow her. He yawns with weariness.)*

Demetrius: There is no following her in this fierce vein. Here, therefore, for a while I will remain. *(He lies down and falls asleep at once, while Oberon turns to chide Puck.)*

Oberon: What hast thou done? Thou hast mistaken quite, and laid the love-juice on some true-love's sight. *(Puck bows his head in shame.)* About the wood go swifter than the wind, and Helena of

Athens look thou find. By some illusion, see thou bring her here. *(From his cloak he takes out the magic flower.)* I'll charm his eyes against she do appear.

Puck: I go, I go...look how I go! Swifter than arrow from the Tartar's bow! *(He whirls off to find Helena and bring her back.)*

Oberon: (Bending over Demetrius, he squeezes the flower-juice on his eyelids.)
Flower of this purple dye,
Hit with Cupid's archery,
Sink in apple of his eye.
When his love he doth espy,
Let her shine as gloriously
As the Venus of the sky.
When thou wakest, if she be by,
Beg of her for remedy.

Puck: (Entering rapidly, he points behind him, where Helena is being pursued by the spell-bound Lysander, who tries to kiss her.)
Captain of our fairy band,
Helena is here at hand.
And the youth, mistook by me,
Pleading for a lover's fee.
Shall we their fond pageant see? *(He laughs.)*
Lord, what fools these mortals be!

Oberon: Stand aside. The noise they make will cause Demetrius to awake! *(They become invisible as Helena and Lysander begin to argue loudly, for she believes still he is making fun of her by pretending to be in love.)*

Lysander: Why should you think that I should woo in scorn? *(Almost in tears, he swears his love.)* Look, when I vow, I weep!

Helena: These vows are Hermia's.

Lysander: I had no judgment when to her I swore.

Helena: Nor none, in my mind, now you give her o'er. *(She thinks he has lost his wits.)*

Lysander: Demetrius loves her, and he loves not you.

(Their voices awaken Demetrius. When he sees Helena, magically he falls in love with her.)

Demetrius: O Helen, goddess, nymph, perfect, divine! *(He gazes into her eyes with rapture.)* To what, my love, shall I compare thine eyne? Crystal is muddy. *(He touches her lips with his fingertips.)* O, how ripe in show thy lips, those kissing cherries, tempting grow!

Helena: *(She sees only more cruel jokes in his love-talk.)* O Spite! O Hell! *(Looking from one man to the other, she believes they have rudely joined together to tease her.)* I see you all are bent to set against me for your merriment. Can you not hate me, as I know you do, but you must join in souls to mock me too? If you were men, as men you are in show, you would not use a gentle lady so. You both are rivals, and love Hermia. And now both rivals to mock Helena!

Lysander: *(Scolding Demetrius, to whom he gives Hermia in return for Helena.)* You are unkind, Demetrius. Be not so. For you love Hermia — this

you know I know. And here, with all good will,
with all my heart, in Hermia's love I yield you up
my part. And yours of Helena to me bequeath,
whom I do love, and will do till my death!

Demetrius: (With equal scorn for Lysander.) Lysander,
keep thy Hermia. I will none. If e'er I loved her, all
that love is gone. My heart to her but as "guest-
wise" sojourned, and now to Helen is it home
returned, there to remain. *(He looks at Helena
ardently.)*

Lysander: (Shouting) Helen, it is not so!

Demetrius: (To Lysander) Look, where thy love comes.
Yonder is thy dear! *(He points towards Hermia,
who comes running to them in relief that her
Lysander is safe. She has found them by their
loud voices.)*

Hermia: Thou art not by mine eye, Lysander, found.
Mine ear, I thank it, brought me to thy sound. But
why unkindly didst thou leave me so? *(She hugs
him, but he does not respond.)*

Lysander: (In a cold voice) Why should he stay, whom
love doth press to go?

Hermia: (Confused) What love could press Lysander
from my side?

Lysander: Lysander's love, that would not let him
bide…*(He pushes her away and kneels before
Helena in the starlight.)*…fair Helena, who more
engilds the night than all yon fiery orbs and eyes
of light. *(To Hermia, with a frown.)* Why seekst

thou me? Could not this make thee know, the **hate** I bare thee made me leave thee so?

Hermia: (She puts her hand to her mouth in astonishment at her changed lover.) You speak not as you think. It cannot be!

Helena: (In the belief that Hermia has joined the men to continue the heartless teasing.) Lo, she is one of this confederacy! Now I perceive they have conjoined, all three, to fashion this false sport in spite of me. *(To her friend)* Injurious Hermia! Most ungrateful maid!

(She appeals to their childhood memories together.) Is all the counsel that we two have shared, the sister's vows — O, is it all forgot? All school days friendship, childhood innocence? We, Hermia, have with our needles created both one flower, sitting on one cushion, both warbling of one song, both in one key. So we grew together, like to a double cherry, seeming parted, but yet an union in partition. Two lovely berries molded on one stem. So, with two seeming bodies, but one heart.

(Pleading for kindness) And will you rend our ancient love asunder, to join with men in scorning your poor friend? It is not friendly. Tis not maidenly.

Hermia: (Bewildered) I am amazed at your passionate words. I scorn you not. It seems that you scorn me.

Helena: (Pointing to Hermia's lovers) Have you not set Lysander, as in scorn, to follow me and praise

my eyes and face? And made your other love,
Demetrius — who, even but now, did spurn me
with his foot — to call me goddess, nymph, divine
and rare, precious, celestial?

Hermia: (She shakes her head.) I understand not what
you mean by this!

Helena: Ay, do! *(She imagines they will laugh at her
when her back is turned.)* Make mouths upon me
when I turn my back, wink at each other, hold the
sweet jest up. But fare ye well. Tis partly my own
fault, which death or absence soon shall remedy.
(She starts to leave, but Lysander stops her.)

Lysander: Stay, gentle Helena. Hear my excuse. *(With
passion)* My love, my life, my soul, fair Helena!

Helena: (Bitterly applauding) O excellent!

Hermia: (To Lysander, thinking still he is joking.)
Sweet, do not scorn her so. *(She tries to tug him
away from Helena.)*

Lysander: Helen, I love thee. By my life, I do! *(He
covers Helena's hand with kisses.)*

Demetrius: I say I love thee more than he can do! *(He
pushes Lysander aside and takes Helena's hand.)*

Lysander: (As he draws his sword.) If thou say so,
withdraw and prove it too.

*Demetrius: (Dropping the girl's hand, he draws his
sword also.)* Quick, come!

*Hermia: (She clings for dear life to Lysander, her
dark eyes flashing tears.)* Lysander, whereto
tends all this?

Lysander: Hang off, thou cat, thou burr! *(He tries to peel her fingers free.)* Vile thing, let loose, or I will shake thee from me like a serpent!

Hermia: Why are you grown so rude! What change is this, sweet love?

Lysander: Thy love! *(He pushes her away and mocks her dark hair.)* Out, tawny Tartar, out!

Hermia: Do you not jest?

Helena: (Scornfully to Hermia) Yes, and so do you.

Lysander: (Still to Hermia) Tis no jest that I do hate thee, and love Helena!

Hermia: (Suddenly erupting in a fury at Helena.) O me! You juggler! You thief of love! What, have you come by night and stolen my love's heart from him?

Helena: (Refusing to quarrel, she draws herself up to her full height above the little spitfire form of Hermia.) What, will you tear impatient answers from my gentle tongue? Fie, fie! You puppet, you!

Hermia: Puppet? Why, so? *(Exploding with anger)* Ay, **that** way goes the game! Now I perceive that she hath made compare between our statures. *(Their difference in size increases the quarrel.)* And are you grown so high in his esteem, because I am so dwarfish and so low? How low am I, thou painted maypole? Speak! How low am I? I am not yet so low but that my nails can reach unto thine eyes. *(She jumps up to scratch at Helena's face.)*

Lysander: Be not afraid. She shall not
    harm thee, Helena!

Helena: (Retreating, she begs the men to help her.) I pray you, though you mock me, gentlemen, let her not hurt me. *(In fear of her little friend.)* Let her not strike me! You perhaps may think, because she is something lower than myself, that I can match her.

Hermia: (With her claws still out-stretched.) "Lower!" Hark again!

Helena: (Fearfully trying to quiet Hermia.) Good Hermia, do not be so bitter with me. I evermore did love you, Hermia. *(She wants to go home.)* And now, so you will let me quiet go, to Athens will I bear my folly back and follow you no further. Let me go!

Lysander: (Standing between the girls to protect Helena.) Be not afraid. She shall not harm thee, Helena!

Demetrius: (Also protecting her) No, sir, she shall not!

Helena: (Peeping over their shoulders at her little schoolmate.) O, when she's angry, she is keen and shrewd! She was a vixen when she went to school. And though she be but little, she is fierce.

Hermia: (Trying to get past the men and scratch Helena's eyes out.) "Little" again! Nothing but "low" and "little"! Let me come to her!

Lysander: (Pushing Hermia away) Get you gone, you dwarf, you bead, you acorn! *(She clings to him, trying to get past him and Demetrius.)*

Demetrius: (To Hermia, warning her with his sword.) Let her alone. Speak not of Helena.

*Lysander: (Shaking free of Hermia, who stands
    stunned, he repeats the challenge to Demetrius to
    fight.)* Now she holds me not. Now follow, if thou
    darest, to try whose right — of thine or mine — is
    most in Helena.

Demetrius: (Flourishing his sword also) Follow? Nay,
    I'll go with thee! *(They leave to find a dueling-
    place, and Helena, now unguarded, starts to slip
    away from fierce little Hermia.)*

Hermia: Nay, go not back! *(She stands in front of the
    path to Athens.)*

Helena: I will not trust you, I. Nor longer stay in your
    curst company. Your hands than mine are quicker
    for a fray. My legs are longer, though, to run away.
    (She darts off farther into the wood.)

Hermia: I am amazed, and know not what to say.
    *(Slowly she follows Helena, and Oberon turns to
    scold Puck, who has been enjoying the lovers'
    quarrels.)*

Oberon: This is thy negligence!

Puck: Believe me, King of Shadows, I mistook.
    (Repeating Oberon's original orders) Did not you
    tell me I should know the man by the Athenian
    garments he had on?

*Oberon: (Ignoring Puck's excuse, he gives new orders
    about the duelists.)* Thou see'st these lovers seek a
    place to fight. *(Puck is to keep the swordsmen
    apart with a magic fog.)* Hie therefore, Robin,
    overcast the night with drooping fog, and lead

these testy rivals so astray as one come not within another's way. *(He gives Puck another plant, an antidote to the love-juice.)* Then crush this herb into Lysander's eye, whose liquor hath this virtuous property — to take from thence all error with his might and make his eyeballs roll with wonted sight.

(He sees a happy end to all troubles.) And back to Athens shall the lovers wend. Whiles I in this affair do thee employ, I'll to my Queen and beg her Indian boy. And then I will her charmed eye release from monster's view, and all things shall be peace.

Puck: *(Seeing the morning star rise in the east.)* My fairy lord, this must be done with haste, for night's swift dragons cut the clouds full fast, and yonder shines Aurora's harbinger...at whose approach, ghosts, wandering here and there, troop home to churchyards, damned spirits all.

Oberon: But we are spirits of another sort. Make no delay. We may effect this business yet ere day.

(King Oberon leaves to steal the Indian child from Titania and cure her lovesick spell for Bottom. Puck, meanwhile, makes ready to tease Demetrius and Lysander before solving their troubles. He sings a little song while he weaves magic fog to confuse the duelists.)

Puck:
Up and down, up and down,
I will lead them up and down.

I am feared in field and town...
Goblin, lead them up and down.
Here comes one!

Lysander: (Entering through the fog with his sword drawn.) Where art thou, proud Demetrius? Speak thou now.

Puck: (Imitating Demetrius' voice) Here, villain, drawn and ready. Where art thou?

Lysander: I will be with thee straight.

Puck: Follow me, then, to plainer ground. *(Lysander blunders past him in the mist, and Demetrius enters, also blinded by the fog.)*

Demetrius: Lysander! Speak again! Thou runaway, thou coward, art thou fled? Speak! In some bush? Where dost thou hide thy head?

Puck: (Imitating Lysander.) Thou coward! Come, thou child! I'll whip thee with a rod!

Demetrius: (Peering through the vapor) Yea, art thou there?

Puck: Follow my voice. *(They exit, Puck gleefully skipping just out of reach of the sword-point.)*

Lysander: (Returning) He goes before me and still dares me on. When I come where he calls, then he is gone. The villain is much lighter-heeled than I. I followed fast, but faster he did fly, that fallen am I in dark, uneven way, and here will rest me. *(He lies down, tired out from the chase.)* Come, thou gentle day! For if but once thou show me thy gray light,

Puck: Ho, ho, ho! Coward!

I'll find Demetrius, and revenge this spite. *(He sleeps, and in a moment in rushes Puck, with Demetrius right behind him. Puck perches in a tree.)*

Puck: Ho, ho, ho! Coward, why comest thou not?

Demetrius: (Looking about blindly) Thou runnst before me, shifting every place and darest not stand, nor look me in the face. Where art thou now?

Puck: Come hither. I am here. *(He dances invisibly around Demetrius, who stops in disgust.)*

Demetrius: Nay, then, thou mockst me. Now, go thy way. *(Sleepy with the chase, he lies down, crying out a last challenge.)* By day's approach, look to be visited! *(He sleeps.)*

Helena: (Entering, tired, her heart sick from those she thinks are enemies.) O weary night, O long and tedious night. I may back to Athens by daylight from these that my poor company detest. And sleep, that sometimes shuts up sorrow's eye, steal me awhile from mine own company. *(In the fog she lies down and sleeps, not seeing the young men. As soon as her eyes close, Puck comes forward to count the sleeping forms.)*

Puck:
Yet but three? Come one more.
Two of both kinds makes up four.
(He looks into the woods.)
Here she comes, curst and sad.
Cupid is a knavish lad,
Thus to make poor females mad.

Hermia: (Step by step she totters in, her garments torn by the thorn bushes.) Never so weary, never so in woe, bedabbled with the dew and torn with briers, I can no further crawl, no further go. My legs can keep no pace with my desires. Here will I rest me till the break of day. *(She lies down and sleeps also.)*

Puck: (Looking at the lovers with satisfaction, he takes the new herb and squeezes the antidote into Lysander's eyes, as he chants his magic spell.)

    On the ground
    Sleep sound.
    I'll apply
    To your eye,
Gentle lover, remedy.
    When thou wakest,
    Thou takest
    True delight
    In the sight
Of thy former lady's eye.
And the country proverb known,
That every man should take his own,
In your waking shall be shown.
    Jack shall have Jill,
    Nought shall go ill,
The man shall have his mare again,
And all shall be well!
(With a giggle and a little wild dance, he flies off.)

ACT IV

Scene 1

(In the same scene, the four lovers lie soundly sleeping as the fog clears. Titania enters with her true-love, Bottom, whose donkey head is now crowned with a circle of flowers. Her fairy folk attend them, and in the background, Oberon watches unseen. Titania leads Bottom towards a bank of flowers while she strokes his hairy cheeks lovingly. He is quite at home now, giving orders to his little servants.)

Titania: Come, sit thee down upon this flowery bed, while I thy amiable cheeks do coy, and stick musk roses in thy sleek smooth head, and kiss thy fair large ears, my gentle joy.

Bottom: (Contentedly) Where's Peaseblossom?

Peaseblossom: (Whisking up with a salute.) Ready!

Bottom: Scratch my head, Peaseblossom. *(His ears wave with pleasure as the elf scratches away, and his big eyes half-close lazily. In an absent-minded manner, he smacks his lips.)* Where's Mounsieur Cobweb?

Cobweb: Ready!

Bottom: Mounsieur Cobweb, good mounsieur, get you your weapons in your hand, and kill me a red-hipped humblebee on the top of a thistle. And,

good mounsieur, bring me the honey bag. And, good mounsieur, have a care the honey bag break not. I would be loath to have you overflown with a honey bag, signior. *(Cobweb flies off.)* Where's Mounsieur Mustardseed?

Mustardseed: Ready! What's your will?

Bottom: Nothing, good mounsieur, but to help Cavalery Cobweb to scratch. *(He claws at his cheeks gently.)* I must to the barber's, mounsieur, for methinks I am marvelous hairy about the face. And I am such a tender ass, if my hair do but tickle me, I must scratch.

Titania: What, wilt thou hear some music, my sweet love?

Bottom: (Nodding with self-satisfaction) I have a reasonable good ear in music. *(He waves one of them.)*

Titania: Or, say, sweet love, what thou desirest to eat.

Bottom: I could munch your good dry oats. Methinks I have a great desire to a bottle of hay. Good hay, sweet hay...*(His voice lengthens out into a donkey's bray, and Titania cuddles closer.)* But, I pray you, let none of your people stir me...*(He yawns mightily.)*...I have an exposition of sleep come upon me.

Titania: Sleep thou, and I will wind thee in my arms. Fairies, be gone, and be all ways away. *(The Fairies depart, and she wraps her arms around him like vines.)* So doth the woodbine, the sweet honeysuckle, gently en-twist. The female ivy so enrings the barky fingers of the elm. O, how I love thee! How I dote on thee! *(Bottom begins to snore with gusto, and she kisses him before she too falls asleep. Oberon comes forward to smile at them. Puck enters and joins him.)*

Oberon: Welcome, good Robin. *(He points to his sleeping Queen and her donkey-love.)* Seest thou this sweet sight? Now I do begin to pity. *(The cause of their quarrel has been settled.)* Meeting her of late behind the wood, I then did ask of her her changeling child, which straight she gave me. And now I have the boy, I will undo this hateful imperfection of her eyes. *(With a gesture at Bottom.)* And, gentle Puck, take this transformed scalp from off the head of this Athenian swain, that, he awaking when the other do, may all to Athens back again repair, and think no more of this night's accidents but as the fierce vexation of a dream.

But first I will release the Fairy Queen. *(He chants as he squeezes the antidote on her eyelids.)*
Be as thou wast wont to be.
See as thou wast wont to see.
Now, my Titania, wake you, my sweet Queen!

Titania: *(Her eyelids fluttering, she sits up and looks at her husband, puzzled.)* My Oberon, what visions have I seen! Methought I was enamored of an ass!

Oberon: *(Chuckling as he points)* There lies your love!

Titania: *(She rises with horror at the sight of Bottom.)* How came these things to pass? Oh!

Oberon: Silence awhile. Robin, take off this head. Titania, music call!

Titania: (A command to the spirits of the air.) Music, ho, music such as charmeth sleep!

Puck: (Removing the donkey's head from Bottom, who still snores happily.) Now, when thou wakest, with thine own fool's eyes peep.

Oberon: (To the invisible musicians.) Sound, music! *(Sweet music begins to play. Oberon smiles at Titania, who smiles back at him.)* Come, my Queen, take hands with me, and rock the ground whereon these sleepers be. *(They dance together in the early morning light, reunited and looking forward to blessing the Duke's wedding also.)*

Now thou and I are new in amity, and will tomorrow midnight solemnly dance in Duke Theseus' house triumphantly and bless it to all fair prosperity. There shall the pairs of faithful lovers be wedded, with Theseus, all in jollity! *(A bird begins to sing.)*

Puck: Fairy King, attend and mark: I do hear the morning lark!

Oberon: Then, my Queen, in silence sad, trip we after night's shade.

Titania: (As they leave to join the shadows.) Come, my lord. And in our flight, tell me how it came this night, that I sleeping here was found, with these mortals on the ground.

(They fly away, as hunting horns sound. Duke Theseus and Hippolyta enter, followed by Egeus

*and the courtiers, all dressed in hunting clothes.
The time has passed magically, and it is the wedding day.)*

Theseus: (To his attendants) Go, one of you, find out
the forester. My love shall hear the music of my
hounds. Let them go! Dispatch, I say, and find
the forester. *(As the attendant leaves, Theseus
smiles at his bride-to-be, for both enjoy the musical baying of the hunting dogs.)* We will, fair
Queen, up to the mountain's top, and mark the
musical confusion of hounds and echo in con-
junction.

*Hippolyta: (Recalling a past hunting scene with
pleasure.)* I was with Hercules and Cadmus once,
when in a wood of Crete, they bayed the bear with
hounds of Sparta. Besides the groves, the skies,
the fountains, every region near seemed all one
mutual cry. I never heard so musical a discord,
such sweet thunder. *(From afar off, the hunting
dogs, chosen for their mellow voices, begin to
sound.)*

Theseus: (With pride) My hounds are bred out of the
Spartan kind. And their heads are hung with ears
that sweep away the morning dew. Crook-kneed
and dewlapped like Thessalian bulls, slow in
pursuit, but matched in mouth like bells. *(They
listen for a moment, until Theseus catches sight of
the sleeping young folk.)* But soft! What nymphs
are these?

Egeus: (In surprise as he inspects each sleeper.) My
lord, this is my daughter here asleep! And this,
Lysander! This, Demetrius is. This Helena, old

Nedar's Helena. *(He shakes his head in disapproval.)* I wonder of their being here together!

Theseus: (Recalling May Day sunrise celebrations.) No doubt they rose up early to observe the rite of May. Is not this the day that Hermia should give answer of her choice?

Egeus: It is, my lord.

Theseus: Go, bid the huntsmen wake them with their horns. *(A courtier shouts to the huntsmen, who wind their horns in a loud cry. The lovers awaken, confused. Theseus looks at them mischievously.)* Good morrow, friends. Saint Valentine is past.

Lysander: Pardon, my lord!

Theseus: I pray you all, stand up. *(They rise, unsure of themselves.)*

Lysander: My lord, I swear I cannot truly say how I came here. But as I think, I came with Hermia hither. Our intent was to be gone from Athens....

Egeus: (In anger) Enough, enough, my lord! You have enough! *(Pointing at Lysander.)* I beg the law, the law upon his head! *(To his favorite young man.)* They would have stolen away, they would, Demetrius!

Demetrius: (To Theseus) My lord, fair Helen told me of their stealth, and I in fury hither followed them, fair Helena in fancy following me. *(He puts his hand to his head, clouded with confusion, as he tells of his change of heart.)* But, my good lord, I wot not by what power, my love to Hermia melted as the snow. And all the faith, the virtue of my heart is only...Helena! *(He takes the astonished Helena in his arms, and she begins to believe his love at last.)*

Theseus: Fair lovers, you are fortunately met. *(Hippolyta whispers in his ear, the Duke nods, and he raises his hand to Egeus, who is stamping about in rage at his daughter's elopement.)* Egeus, I will over-bear your will, for in the Temple, by and by, with us these couples shall eternally be knit.

(Egeus, over-ruled by the Duke, tries to look happy at the honor of having his daughter and the others included in the royal wedding.) Away with us to Athens! *(To the other lovers)* Three and three — we'll hold a feast in great solemnity. Come, Hippolyta! *(He leaves with his smiling bride and the excited courtiers.)*

Demetrius: (Still half-asleep, he looks about puzzled.) These things seem small and undistinguishable, like far-off mountains turned into clouds. Are you sure that we are awake? It seems to me that yet we sleep. We dream. Do not you think the Duke was here, and bid us follow him?

Hermia: (Slowly) Yea, and my father...

Helena: ...and Hippolyta...

Lysander: ...and he did bid us follow to the Temple. *(They stand astonished at their good luck, and suddenly they all join in laughter. Demetrius, without his usual frown, is now as charming as the rest.)*

Demetrius: Why, then, we are awake! Let's follow him, and by the way let us recount our dreams.

(They leave to be married in the Temple of Diana with the Duke and Hippolyta. For a moment all is quiet in the magic wood. Then still half-hidden in his bed of flowers, Bottom slowly stirs. He wears his own face again, and he dreams he is rehearsing.)

Bottom: When my cue comes, call me, and I will answer. My next is "Most fair Pyramus...." *(He opens his eyes and looks about, calling to his friends.)* Heigh-ho, Peter Quince! Flute the bellows-mender? Snout the tinker? Starveling! *(He rubs his head in amazement that his friends have abandoned him while he was dozing.)* God's my life, stolen hence and left me asleep?

(He blinks his eyes, trying to remember.) I have had a dream. past the wit of man to say what dream it was. *(He pats his body.)* Methought I was...there is no man can tell what. Methought I was...*(He feels the top of his head for donkey's ears.)*...and methought I had....*(He feels for his donkey's nose that is not there. It is too much for him, and he shakes his head, scrambling his words badly.)*

The eye of man hath not heard, the ear of man hath not seen, man's hand is not able to taste, his tongue to conceive, nor his heart to report what my dream was. *(With inspiration)* I will get Peter Quince to write a ballad of this dream. It shall be

called "Bottom's Dream," because it hath no bottom! And I will sing it in the latter end of a play before the Duke! *(He leaves hurriedly for Athens and his good friends.)*

ACT V

Scene 1

(In the palace of Theseus, the Duke, his bride, and the courtiers come from the triple wedding in the Temple of Diana and the feast that followed. The Duke and Duchess have just heard the story of the lovers lost in the wood. Hippolyta looks puzzled, but Theseus accepts the story with kindly disbelief.)

Hippolyta: Tis strange, my Theseus, that these lovers speak of.

Theseus: More strange than true. I never believe these antique fables nor these fairy toys. *(He laughs at the unreasonable story told by the crazy sweethearts.)* Lovers and madmen have such seething brains, such shaping fantasies that apprehend more than cool reason ever comprehends.

(He thinks three types of people are most imaginative.) The lunatic, the lover and the poet are of imagination all compact. One sees more devils than vast Hell can hold — that is the madman. *(He chuckles at the lover, who can imagine a Helen of Troy in a gypsy girl.)* The lover, all as frantic, sees Helen's beauty in a brow of Egypt.

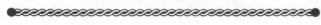

(The poet makes real events out of thin air.) The poet's eye, in a fine frenzy rolling, doth glance from heaven to earth, from earth to heaven. And as imagination bodies forth the forms of things unknown, the poet's pen turns them to shapes, and gives to airy "nothing" a local habitation and a name. Such tricks hath strong imagination!

Hippolyta: (Unable to see how the lovers could dream the same dream unless it really happened.) But all the story of the night told over, and all their minds transfigured so together grows to something of great constancy, but, howsoever, strange and admirable.

Theseus: (Seeing the newly-wedded young couples enter.) Here come the lovers, full of joy and mirth. *(He takes their hands in welcome.)* Joy and fresh days of love accompany your hearts!

Lysander: (Returning the wish of happiness even more.) More than to us wait in your royal walks, your board, your bed!

Theseus: (As they all sit, ready for the evening's entertainment.) Come now, what masques, what dances shall we have, to wear away this long age of three hours between our after-supper and bedtime? Where is our usual manager of mirth? Is there no play to ease the anguish of a torturing hour? Call Philostrate! *(The Master of Ceremonies comes from among the other courtiers.)*

Philostrate: Here, mighty Theseus.

Theseus: Say, what masque? What music? How shall we beguile the lazy time if not with some delight?

Philostrate: (He hands the Duke a list of available entertainment.) Make choice of which your Highness will see first.

Theseus: (Reading the titles, he rejects most of the acts.) "The battle with the Centaurs, to be sung by an Athenian eunuch to the harp." We'll none of that. "The riot of the tipsy Bacchanals, tearing the Thracian singer in their rage." *(He makes a face at the stage show, which he has already seen.)* That is an old device, and it was played when I from Thebes came last a conqueror. "The thrice three Muses mourning for the death of Learning, late deceased in beggary." *(The idea sounds too full of bitter jokes for a celebration.)* That is some satire, keen and critical, not sorting with a nuptial ceremony.

"A tedious brief scene of young Pyramus and his love Thisby, very tragical mirth." *(Theseus looks up from the paper questioningly at Philostrate, for the description contradicts itself.)* Merry and tragical? Tedious and brief? *(He shakes his head at such opposite terms.)* That is, "hot ice"?

Philostrate: (Trying to explain that the tragedy is so bad it is funny.) A play there is, my lord, some ten words long, which is as brief as I have known a play. But by ten words, my lord, it is too long, which makes it tedious. For in all the play, there is not one word apt, one player fitted. And tragical, my noble lord, it is, for Pyramus therein doth kill himself. *(He begins to chuckle at the memory, wiping the tears of laughter from his eyes.)* Which, when I saw rehearsed, I must confess, made mine

eyes water...but more merry tears the passion of loud laughter never shed.

Theseus: What are they that do play it?

Philostrate: Hard-handed men, that work in Athens here, which never labored in their minds till now. And now have toiled their memories with this same play against your nuptial.

Theseus: And we will hear it! *(The others laugh in agreement.)*

Philostrate: (With an attempt to keep the entertainment dignified.) No, my noble lord. It is not for you. I have heard it over, and it is nothing, nothing in the world.

Theseus: I will hear that play! *(He is grateful to his subjects for taking the trouble to try to produce the show.)* For never anything can be amiss, when simpleness and duty tender it. Go, bring them in. And take your places, ladies. *(Philostrate leaves to call the actors, while the courtiers find seats to one side.)*

Hippolyta: (Worried that the actors cannot perform.) He says they can do nothing in this kind.

Theseus: The kinder we, to give them thanks for nothing. *(He intends to be polite at least.)* Our sport shall be to take what they mistake.

Philostrate: (Entering and bowing) So please your Grace, the Prologue is addressed.

Theseus: Let him approach.

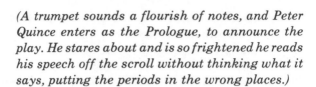

(A trumpet sounds a flourish of notes, and Peter Quince enters as the Prologue, to announce the play. He stares about and is so frightened he reads his speech off the scroll without thinking what it says, putting the periods in the wrong places.)

Quince: (Reading) If we offend, it is with our good will. That you should think, we come not to offend, but with good will. To show our simple skill, that is the true beginning of our end. Our true intent is. All for your delight, we are not here. That you should here repent you, the actors are at hand. And, by their show, you shall know all that you are like to know. *(He bows with a sort of bob to show he has finished.)*

Theseus: His speech was like a tangled chain...all disordered. Who is next? *(The actors now enter: Pyramus and Thisby and Wall and Moonshine and Lion, waiting to be introduced.)*

Quince: (Addressing the gentlefolk) Gentles, perchance you wonder at this show. But wonder on, till truth make all things plain. This man is Pyramus, if you would know. *(Bottom, dressed in Greek armor, bows.)* This beauteous lady Thisby is certain. *(Flute, looking tall and skinny in his Greek lady's dress, curtsies, showing his hairy legs. The stuffing on his chest gives him some trouble, as it has a tendency to slip down to his waist. He gives it a hitch upwards as Quince continues, motioning for Wall to come forward.)*

This man, with lime and roughcast, doth present Wall, that vile Wall which did these lovers sunder. *(Wall bows, holding his trowel and mortar in one*

hand. He is dressed in a square box painted to represent stones. He holds out his free hand, two fingers spread wide apart, as Prologue continues.) And through Wall's chink, poor souls, they are content to whisper. At the which, let no man wonder.

(Moonshine comes forward, dragging a stuffed dog, and shines his lantern at the audience.) This man, with lantern, dog and bush of thorn, presenteth Moonshine! For, if you will know, by moonshine did these lovers think no scorn to meet at Ninus' tomb, there, there to woo.

(Prologue beckons to Lion, who comes forward in a moth-eaten fur rug. Below the lion mask can be seen the stupid face of Snug the joiner.) This grisly beast, which Lion hight by name, the trusty Thisby, coming first by night, did scare away, or rather did affright. And, as she fled, her mantle she did fall…*(Thisby drops her cloak to illustrate.)*…which Lion vile with bloody mouth did stain. *(Lion chews on the cloak and growls.)* Anon comes Pyramus, sweet youth and tall, and finds his trusty Thisby's mantle slain.

(Quince takes a deep breath, for he is getting to the important suicide part with the great big words.) Whereat, with blade, with bloody blameful blade, he bravely broached his boiling bloody breast! And Thisby, tarrying in mulberry shade, his dagger drew, and died. For all the rest, let Lion, Moonshine, Wall and lovers twain at large discourse, while here they do remain. *(Having told*

the whole plot and ruined any suspense, Quince
bows and smiles while the audience applauds.)

Theseus: (In a whisper to the others.) I wonder if the
lion be to speak.

Demetrius: (Whispering back) No wonder, my lord.
One lion may when many asses do!

(*They watch Lion, Thisby and Moonshine leave.
Pyramus stands off to one side, waiting, and
Quince nervously holds the promptbook. Wall
comes forward and bows as much as his box-
costume will allow. In plain speech, the Wall
addresses the audience and tells all over again
what he is.*)

Wall: (He holds out his fingers spread apart.) In this
same interlude it doth befall that I, one Snout by
name, present a wall. And such a wall, as I would
have you think, that had in it a crannied hole or
chink, through which the lovers, Pyramus and
Thisby, did whisper often very secretly. *(He waves
his holder about, the mortar almost slides off, so
he pushes it back.)* This loam, this rough-cast and
this stone doth show that I am that same wall.
The truth is so. *(He extends again his two spread
fingers.)* And this the cranny is, right and sinister,
through which the fearful lovers are to whisper.

Theseus: (To the others of the audience.) Would you
desire lime and hair to speak better?

Demetrius: It is the wittiest partition that ever I heard,
my lord.

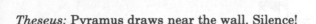

Theseus: Pyramus draws near the wall. Silence!

*Pyramus: (Bottom's big voice booms out in the worst of
ham-acting as he gives himself wholly to his part.
He strides about the stage looking at the sky.)* O
grim-looked night! O night with hue so black! O
night, which ever art when day is not! O night, O
night! *(He slaps his forehead, knocking his helmet
sideways.)* Alack, alack, alack! I fear my Thisby's
promise is forgot! *(Straightening his helmet, he
strides to the Wall.)* And thou, O Wall, O sweet, O
lovely Wall, that stand'st between her father's
ground and mine...*(Wall nods and shakes hands
with Pyramus.)*...thou Wall, O Wall, O sweet and
lovely Wall, show me thy chink, to blink through
with mine eyne!

*(Wall holds up his fingers, and Pyramus bends
down to look through.)* Thanks, courteous Wall.
Jove shield thee well for this! *(Wall smiles in
appreciation, and Pyramus peers between the
fingers. He sees nothing, and he takes a step
backwards in shock.)* But what see I? No Thisby
do I see! *(He straightens up and frowns at Wall.)* O
wicked Wall, through whom I see no bliss! *(Wall
looks apologetic.)* Cursed be thy stones for thus
deceiving me!

Theseus: The wall, methinks, being sensible, should
curse again.

*Pyramus: (He stops acting and walks over to the Duke
to explain about the play.)* No, in truth, sir, he
should not. "Deceiving me" is Thisby's cue. She is
to enter now, and I am to spy her through the wall.
You shall see it will fall pat as I told you. Yonder
she comes! *(Flute enters, tripping over his scarf*

Thisby: I kiss the Wall's hole, not your
lips at all!

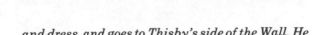

and dress, and goes to Thisby's side of the Wall. He speaks — or rather shrieks — in such a high voice it cracks at times.)

Thisby: O Wall, full often hast thou heard my moans, for parting my fair Pyramus and me! My cherry lips have often kissed thy stones, thy stones with lime and hair knit up in thee.

Pyramus: (His hand to his ear, he begins to scramble his lines.) I see a voice! Now will I to the chink, to spy and I can hear my Thisby's face! *(Bending to the chink, he calls out.)* Thisby!

Thisby: (As she bends also, her bosom-stuffing starts to slide out of the costume, and she adjusts her figure while speaking to Pyramus.) My love thou art, my love I think.

Pyramus: Think what thou wilt. I am thy lover's grace. *(Wall starts to watch the audience, and slowly his hand begins to drop so Pyramus and Thisby bend lower and lower, falling to their knees.)* O kiss me through the hole of this vile wall!

Thisby: (Kissing Wall's fingers with a loud smack and exclaiming in maidenly dismay.) I kiss the Wall's hole, not your lips at all!

Pyramus: (Almost on the floor because of Wall's descending hand, Pyramus jerks Wall's hand up and holds it steady. He spits out his words.) Wilt thou at Ninny's tomb meet me straightway? *(Wall wipes the spit from his hand and puts his fingers out again.)*

Thisby: Tide life, tide death, I come without delay. *(Pyramus strides off his side of the stage, and*

Thisby daintily holds her skirts high over her hairy legs and trips off her side of the stage. Wall comes forward and bows.)

Wall: Thus have I, Wall, my part discharged so. And, being done, thus Wall away doth go. *(He walks off stiffly to the audience's applause.)*

Hippolyta: This is the silliest stuff that ever I heard!

Theseus: (Excusing the actors) The best in this kind are but shadows. And the worst are no worse, if imagination amend them. *(He sees Lion and Moonshine enter.)* Here come two noble beasts in, a man and a lion.

Lion: (Speaking slowly in a dim-witted fashion.) You ladies, you, whose gentle hearts do fear the smallest monstrous mouse that creeps on floor, may now perchance both quake and tremble here, when Lion rough in wildest rage doth roar. *(He pulls his headdress half-off to show his face.)* Then know that I, as Snug the joiner, am a lion fell, nor else no lion's dam.

Theseus: A very gentle beast, and of a good conscience!

Demetrius: The very best at a beast, my lord, that e'er I saw!

Theseus: It is well. Let us listen to the Moon.

(Starveling, playing Moonshine, comes forward and bobs a timid bow, holding up his lantern, his thornbush and his stuffed dog, which were supposed to be with the Man in the Moon. He tries to explain his lantern is a crescent moon with two points.)

Moonshine: This lanthorn doth the
hornèd moon present...

Moonshine: This lanthorn doth the hornèd moon present...

Demetrius: (Interrupting) He should have worn the horns on his head.

Theseus: He is no crescent, and his horns are invisible within the circumference.

Moonshine: (Starting his speech again) This lanthorn doth the hornèd moon present. Myself the Man in the Moon do seem to be.

Theseus: (Interrupting) This is the greatest error of all the rest. The man should be put **into** the lantern. How is it else the Man in the Moon?

Demetrius: (Peering into the open door of the lantern.) He dares not come there for the candle!

Hippolyta: I am weary of this moon. Would he would change!

Lysander: Proceed, Moon.

Moonshine: (Almost foaming at the interruptions, he stammers out his speech.) All that I have to say is to tell you that the lanthorn is the moon; I, the Man in the Moon; this thorn bush, my thorn bush; and this dog, my dog. *(He jerks at the stuffed dog. It flies up and hits him in the face.)*

Demetrius: Why, all these should be in the lantern, for all these are in the moon, But, silence! Here comes Thisby.

Thisby: (Entering and staring about her.) This is old Ninny's tomb. Where is my love?

Lion: (Roars) Oh! *(Thisby runs off, dropping her cloak. Everyone applauds loudly.)*

Demetrius: Well roared, Lion!

Theseus: Well run, Thisby!

Hippolyta: Well shone, Moon! Truly, the Moon shines with a good grace. *(Moonshine smiles, happy at last. The Lion, roaring again, shakes Thisby's mantle with his mouth, spits it out, and exits.)*

Theseus: Well moused, Lion!

Demetrius: And then came Pyramus.

Lysander: And so the Lion vanished.

Pyramus: (Entering and waving heartily to Moonshine, who waves back.) Sweet Moon, I thank thee for thy sunny beams. I thank thee, Moon, for shining now so bright. For, by thy gracious, golden, glittering gleams, I trust to take of truest Thisby sight. *(He sees Thisby's cloak.)*
But stay, O spite!
But mark, poor knight,
What dreadful dole is here!
(He looks at the bloodstains that were left by Lion's bloody mouth.)
O dainty duck! O dear!
Thy mantle good,
What, stained with blood!
(He shouts in tragical sorrow to the heavens.)
Approach, ye Furies fell!
O, Fates, come, come,
Cut thread and thrum!
Quail, crush, conclude, and quell!

Theseus: (Laughing behind his hand) This passion
and the death of a dear friend would go near to
make a man look sad.

Hippolyta: (Laughing in spite of herself.) Beshrew
my heart, but I pity the man.

Pyramus: (With loud weeping at his tragic loss.)
O wherefore, Nature, did'st thou lions frame?
   Since lion vile hath here deflowered my dear:
Which is…no, no,…which **was** the fairest dame
   That lived, that loved, that liked, that looked
      with cheer.
      Come, tears, confound. *(He draws his sword.)*
      Out, sword and wound
   The pap of Pyramus. *(He beats at his left chest.)*
      Ay, that left pap,
      Where heart doth hop! *(He stabs himself
      several times.)*

   Thus die I, thus, thus, thus…*(He lies down, the
   sword held between his chest and arm. He raises
   his head to add more.)*

   Now am I dead,
   Now am I fled.
My soul is in the sky. *(He waves good-by to it.)*
   Tongue, lose thy light.
   Moon, take thy flight. *(Moonshine exits.)*
Now die, die, die, die, die. *(He lays his head on the
floor and closes his eyes.)*

Hippolyta: (Wiping away her tears of laughter.) How
chance Moonshine is gone before Thisby comes
back and finds her lover?

Theseus: She will find him by starlight. Here she comes, and her passion ends the play. *(Thisby trips in daintily and looks about.)*

Hippolyta: I hope she will be brief.

Lysander: (As Thisby sees Pyramus and throws her hands high in horror.) She hath spied him already with those sweet eyes!

Thisby: (Squeaking) Asleep, my love? *(She raises Pyramus' head and drops it heavily onto the floor. It makes a loud thump.)*
  What, dead, my dove?
  O Pyramus, arise! *(She thumps his head on the floor several times.)*
    Speak, speak. Quite dumb?
    Dead, dead? A tomb
  Must cover thy sweet eyes. *(She pokes at his face.)*
    These lily lips,
    This cherry nose,
  These yellow cowslip cheeks,
    Are gone, are gone.
    Lovers, make moan.
  His eyes were green as leeks! *(She cries out to the Fates as she shoves her slipping bosom back into place.)*
    O Sisters Three,
    Come, come to me,
  With hands as pale as milk.
    Lay them in gore
    Since you have shore
  With shears his thread of silk.
    Tongue, not a word.

Thisby: What, dead, my dove?

Come, trusty sword...*(She attempts to withdraw Pyramus' sword from his side, but he forgets to release it, and Thisby has a tug-of-war with the corpse over it. At last Pyramus lets go, sending Thisby stumbling away across the floor. Her bosom slides down to her waist, and she grabs the stuffing and proceeds to stab it.)*

Come, blade, my breast imbrue! *(With a last stab, she throws away the sword and blows farewell kisses to the audience.)*

And farewell, friends.

Thus Thisby ends.

Adieu, adieu, adieu! *(With a final screech, she flings herself across the body of Pyramus and dies. The audience applauds loudly.)*

Theseus: Moonshine and Lion are left to bury the dead.

Demetrius: Ay, and Wall too.

Bottom: (Starting up from under the corpse of dead Thisby.) No, I assure you. The Wall is down that parted their fathers. *(Thisby also rises, a little embarrassed, and bows to the audience as Bottom continues, happy at their applause.)* Will it please you to see the epilogue, or to hear a Bergomask dance between two of our company?

Theseus: No epilogue, I pray you. For your play needs no excuse. Never excuse, for when the players are all dead, there need none to be blamed. *(With a joke that the playwright should be killed.)* Marry, if he that writ it had played Pyramus and hanged himself in Thisby's garter, it would have been a fine tragedy...*(Bottom looks puzzled, and the Duke hastens to reassure him that the play has*

indeed been very fine.) And so it is, truly, and very
notable discharged. But, come, your Bergomask.
Let your epilogue alone. *(Bottom smiles widely as
the Duke gives him a heavy bag of silver for all the
acting company, a final proof of success.)*

*(Bowing to further applause, Bottom and Thisby
go offstage. Two rustic dancers come forward and
do a peasant dance, also heartily applauded. At
the end, the clock strikes. The Duke rises, takes his
bride by the hand, and bids all good-night.)*

The iron tongue of midnight hath told twelve.
Lovers, to bed. Tis almost fairy time! I fear we
shall outsleep the coming morn. Sweet friends, to
bed. *(He promises two more weeks of celebration.)*
A fortnight hold we this solemnity, in nightly
revels and new jollity!

*(All leave in a magnificent procession, as the
servants put out the candles. Moonlight floods the
empty chamber. Then from around a curtain
comes Puck with a broom, which he uses to sweep
the hall, as a gesture of good fellowship.)*

Puck:
Now the hungry lion roars,
    And the wolf be-howls the moon.
Whilst the heavy plowman snores,
    All with weary task fordone.
Now it is the time of night
    That the graves, all gaping wide,
Every one lets forth his sprite,
    In the churchway paths to glide.

Fairies frolic! Not a mouse
   Shall disturb this hallowed house.
I am sent, with broom, before,
To sweep the dust behind the door.
*(Oberon and Titania and all their elves and fairies
enter, to make music and to bless the house with
the newlyweds within it.)*

Oberon:

Through the house give glimmering light
   By the dead and drowsy fire:
Every elf and fairy sprite
   Hop as light as bird from brier.
And this ditty, after me,
Sing and dance it trippingly.

Titania:

First, rehearse your song by rote,
To each word a warbling note:
Hand in hand, with fairy grace,
Will we sing, and bless this place!
(All the fairy-folk sing and dance.)

Oberon: *(Giving orders for the fairy blessing of the
   palace.)*
Now, until the break of day
Through this house each fairy stray.
So shall all the couples three
Ever true in loving be.
Every fairy take his gait
And each several chamber bless
Through this palace, with sweet peace.
And the owner of it blest
Ever shall in safety rest.

Oberon:
And each several chamber bless
Through this palace, with sweet
peace.

Trip away. Make no stay.
Meet me all by break of day!

(The fairies leave to scatter dewdrops and bless-
ings about. Puck is left alone, and he comes to-
wards the theatre audience to speak an epilogue or
apology: if the audience is not satisfied, they can
think the play is only a dream. And if pardoned,
the actors will try to improve and mend their
ways.)

Puck:
If we shadows have offended,
Think but this, and all is mended:
That you have but slumbered here,
While these visions did appear.
And this weak and idle theme
No more yielding but a dream.
Gentles, do not reprehend.
If you pardon, we will mend.
And, as I am an honest Puck,
If we have unearned luck
Now to 'scape the serpent's tongue,
We will make amends ere long.
Else the Puck a liar call.
So, good night unto you all! *(Bowing in hope of*
    applause.)
Give me your hands, if we be friends,
And Robin shall restore amends!
(To the last applause, he skips off.)

FINIS

SOME FAMOUS QUOTATIONS

Lysander: The course of true love never did run smooth. *(Act I, Scene 1)*

Lysander: ...the jaws of darkness do devour it up. So quick bright things come to confusion. *(Act I, Scene 1)*

Helena: Love looks not with the eyes but with the mind, and therefore is winged Cupid painted blind. *(Act I, Scene 1)*

Bottom: ...a part to tear a cat in. *(Act I, Scene 2)*

Bottom: Let **me** play the lion too!...I will roar, that I will make the Duke say, "Let him roar again!" *(Act I, Scene 2)*

Fairy: Over hill, over dale, thorough bush, thorough brier. *(Act II, Scene 1)*

Oberon: Ill met by moonlight, proud Titania! *(Act II, Scene 1)*

Oberon: ...once I sat upon a promontory, and heard a mermaid, on a dolphin's back, uttering such dulcet and harmonious breath that the rude sea grew civil at her song, and certain stars shot madly from their spheres, to hear the sea maid's music. *(Act II, Scene 1)*

Oberon: But the imperial votress passed on in maiden meditation, fancy-free. *(Act II, Scene 1)*

Puck: I'll put a girdle round about the earth in forty minutes! *(Act II, Scene 1)*

Oberon: I know a bank where the wild thyme blows. *(Act II, Scene 1)*

Puck: What hempen homespuns have we swaggering here? *(Act III, Scene 1)*

Bottom: And yet, to say the truth, reason and love keep little company together nowadays. *(Act III, Scene 1)*

Puck: I go, I go...look how I go! Swifter than arrow from the Tartar's bow! *(Act III, Scene 2)*

Puck: Lord, what fools these mortals be! *(Act III, Scene 2)*

Helena: So we grew together, like to a double cherry, seeming parted, but yet an union in partition. Two lovely berries molded on one stem. *(Act III, Scene 2)*

Puck: Jack shall have Jill, Nought shall go ill, The man shall have his mare again, And all shall be well! *(Act III, Scene 2)*

Hippolyta: Besides the groves, the skies, the fountains, every region near seemed all one mutual cry. I never heard so musical a discord, such sweet thunder. *(Act IV, Scene 1)*

Bottom: Methought I was...and methought I had... *(Act IV, Scene 1)*

Theseus: Lovers and madmen have such seething brains...The lunatic, the lover and the poet are of imagination all compact...And as imagination bodies forth the forms of things unknown, the poet's pen turns them to shapes, and gives to airy "nothing" a local habitation and a name. *(Act V, Scene 1)*

Pyramus: I see a voice!...I can hear my Thisby's face! *(Act V, Scene 1)*

Pyramus: O dainty duck! O dear! *(Act V, Scene 1)*

Pyramus: Ay, that left pap, Where heart doth hop! *(Act V, Scene 1)*

Theseus: The iron tongue of midnight hath told twelve. Lovers, to bed. Tis almost fairy time! *(Act V, Scene 1)*